D1666771

Scandinavian
cooking

Scandinavian
cooking

Sonia Maxwell

Quantum
Books

A QUANTUM BOOK

This book is produced by
Quantum Publishing Ltd.
6 Blundell Street
London N7 9BH

Copyright ©MCMXCV
Quintet Publishing Ltd.

This edition printed 2005

All rights reserved.
This book is protected by copyright. No part of it
may be reproduced, stored in a retrieval system, or
transmitted in any form or by any means, without
the prior permission in writing of the Publisher, nor
be otherwise circulated in any form of binding or
cover other than that in which it is published and
without a similar condition including this condition
being imposed on the subsequent publisher.

ISBN 1-84573-035-6

QUMSDC

This book is produced by
Quantum Publishing Ltd
6 Blundell Street
London N7 9BH

Picture credits
The publishers would like to thank the following
organizations for supplying pictures of Scandinavia.
Danish Tourist Board:pages 1 (D.Betz), 13 (O.
Akhof), 51 (D. Betz), 77 (D. Betz), 113 (Mayher)
Finish Tourist Board: pages 7, 12, 18, 31, 66
Life File: pages 6 (Cecilia Innes), 10 Nigel
Shuttleworth), 21 (Richard Powers), 65 (Eric Wilkins),
75 (Cecilia Innes), 79 (F.Ralston), 111 (Andrew
Ward), 121 (Terry O'Brien)
Norwegian Tourist Board: Pages 9, 33, 82, 95
Swedish Travel and Tourism Council: pages 11
(Göran Assner), 54 (Per Klaesson)

Typeset in Great Britain by
Central Southern Typesetters, Eastbourne
Manufactured in Malaysia by C.H. Colour Scan Sdn.
Bhd
Printed in Singapore by
Star Standard Industries (Pte) Ltd.

CONTENTS

SCANDINAVIA – LAND OF THE MIDNIGHT SUN

Sweden, Finland, Norway, and Denmark form the most northerly region of Europe, Scandinavia – a region that has seen many political alliances: Sweden united with Norway and Denmark; Sweden with Finland; Denmark with Norway. So it is easy to understand the influence each of these countries has had upon its neighbors. Their shared traditions, customs, and cuisines can be traced back to the Vikings. However, they are four entirely independent countries, each of which has retained unique and unmistakable characteristics.

The people of the north are as different from each other as the lands in which they dwell, but they share a love of nature. The great distances that separate communities in the sparsely populated countryside of Sweden, Norway, and Finland, and the 150,000 lakes that break up Sweden's land mass, have also given the people a taste for silence and solitude. Forests stretch north to Lapland, where they peter out and eventually make way for vast wastelands of ice and snow. The people may seem reserved on first meeting, but, once the ice is broken, it is easy to see how they gained their high-spirited and easy-going reputation. The need to contend with natural elements has made them excel at sports such as skiing, ice-skating, canoeing, fishing, and sailing.

Because of its latitude, Scandinavia's seasonal pattern is unique, and it is the hours of daylight rather than the temperature that determine the change of season. In some regions there may be 19 hours of daylight on a summer day, and people enjoy the long evenings outdoors: in June and July there is no night in Lapland. Winter brings snow and long hours of darkness, and the fireplace is at its most inviting at this time of year. When the sun sets in the depth of winter, it does not rise again for another 51 days.

The Vikings were hospitable people who left a door open for the unexpected guest, and hospitality is still a characteristic of Scandinavians today. Scandinavians have also gained a reputation for good design. They spend a great deal of time in their homes and have become expert at furnishing their dwellings comfortably. Their imaginative table settings for entertaining are renowned, and it follows that people who take such care in presentation should also care about food. This is illustrated by the attention lavished on the delicacies that make up the *smörgåsbord,* one of the better-known preparations of the Scandinavian kitchen.

Scandinavian cuisine can be described as complicated, varied, and in harmony with nature – the key to the Nordic table being the climate. To survive the long winters, people had to store supplies. As a result, every possible method of preservation was used to produce a selection of dried, smoked, and cured meat and fish, unmatched anywhere else. The Vikings took these preserves with them on their long voyages to distant lands for sustenance, and as a means of bargaining. Local produce has always formed the basis of Scandinavian cuisine, and game is used extensively (bear, reindeer, elk, snow grouse, and snow hare). The sea is also a great provider, and crayfish, lobster, oysters, mussels, herrings, trout, salmon, and cod are abundant.

The lavish interior of the Stockholm Opera café.

When salt was too expensive or in short supply, other means of preserving had to be found – meat would be stored in butter or whey, and fish was sometimes buried in a crude attempt at refrigeration. The fish often fermented, and this was considered a delicacy. Swedish *surstromming,* a Baltic herring preparation based on this practice, is one dish that still survives today.

But salt has always been a favorite condiment, and, in times gone by, when the price of salt dropped and people found it once again affordable, they would use it with such zeal in the preservation of food that violent thirsts were commonplace. Although salt is no longer used so liberally, Scandinavians still have a taste for salty foods. Many recipes use fresh meat that has been boiled in brine and left to soak for days to impart flavor and tenderize it.

Herring and cod are hung up and left to dry in the brisk Atlantic wind. Dried cod, known as "stokkfisk," is later made into "lutefisk" by soaking it in a lye (alkaline) solution before cooking. Because cod and herring are so readily available and so easily preserved, they have become two of Scandinavia's principal sources of food, and major exports. Dried and salt cod preparations introduced to Portugal, Spain, and Italy by the Vikings during their voyages to Southern Europe have remained popular in these countries.

Smoking houses provided a wide range of smoked meats and fish for the Scandinavian table, but the Vikings also savored mutton, cabbage, apples, cheese, cucumber, horseradish, mushrooms, nuts, and berries – all of which continue to feature in the Scandinavian diet. Parsley and dill, in particular, are used extensively to flavor and garnish dishes. Other staple foods include a variety of cultured milks (fresh milk is a popular drink), fresh and soured cream, and salted butter. The range of crispbreads and flatbreads available is as wide as that of leavened bread. Moisture content of crispbreads and flatbreads is low in order to ensure good keeping qualities, and some have a hole in the center so they can be hung from the rafter to keep them dry.

Scandinavians like to precede or accompany their food with the strong liqueur, aquavit, and beer. Norwegian beer is good and regularly enjoyed in Norway – it is also exported to the United States. Beers range from strong "Easter" beers (8 percent alcohol) to lighter varieties to quench a summer thirst. Although aquavit is enjoyed throughout Scandinavia, each nation has its favorite ritual or particular way of serving the liqueur. The Danes like a strong, piping hot coffee with aquavit. It can also be served in chilled, long-stemmed glasses and downed in one. A

The sea is an important provider of fish for all the Scandinavian countries.

toast in aquavit is a solemn procedure, involving looking your companion in the eye, saying "Skal," and emptying your glass in one. Aquavit is not the only spirit enjoyed in Scandinavia: scotch and gin are popular in Norway and, with Russia on their eastern border, it is not surprising that the Finns like vodka.

Fresh garden produce, salads, berries, fruits, fresh fish, often plump with roe, and creamy dairy products are the foods of summer, when most meals are eaten outdoors to take full advantage of the long daylight hours. As winter closes in, people turn to their cozy, comfortable homes and flickering candlelight adds warmth and color. Game and mushrooms from the forest, simmering stews, and home-baked breads grace the table as the days become shorter.

To delve into Scandinavian cuisine is to take a journey through its countryside, and perhaps to catch a glimpse of its people. Dishes vary with the region, but each has a special significance and sometimes a story to tell.

N

*Norwegian
Sea*

FINNMARK

RUSSIA

*Gulf
of
Bothnia*

FINLAND

NORWAY

SWEDEN

Oslo •

• *Stockholm*

• *Helsinki*

• *Stavanger*

ESTONIA

Goteborg •

*North
Sea*

*Baltic
Sea*

LATVIA

DENMARK

LITHUANIA

• *Copenhagen*

GERMANY

POLAND

SCANDINAVIA

NORWAY

The scenery in Norway can only be described as dramatic. It is a land of high, snow-capped mountains, fjords cut deep into the coastline, and virgin forest teeming with wildlife. Here you can only marvel at the toughness of a land where only 4 percent of the ground can be cultivated.

Norwegians love the outdoor life, and retreat to their "hytter," or cabins, to escape from the stress of modern times. Here they hunt, fish, pick wild berries and mushrooms, and enjoy nature's bounty. They are a resilient people who enjoy hiking in summer and skiing in winter. However, they retain a healthy respect for the mountainous landscape, leaving vast areas of the country untouched.

Norwegians are proud of their Viking ancestors, who first united the country in the 8th century, but for the next thousand years the country was under the rule of either Denmark or Sweden. Full independence was only achieved in 1905, despite the fact that the constitution was written in 1814. The 19th century produced many of Norway's great names – the composer Edvard Grieg, dramatist Henrik Ibsen, artist Edvard Munch, and polar explorer Roald Amundsen among them.

Winters are relatively mild along the coast, particularly in the south of the country – the Gulf Stream usually keeps the temperature in Oslo no lower than –20°F. Inland and farther north it is a different story – winters are long, very cold, and very dark. Summers are mild, but the temperature can drop sharply at night.

Due to the need to keep out the cold, Norwegians have long regarded food as fuel. Breakfast tends to be substantial, with herring, cold meats, and cheese served with crusty bread. Lunch breaks are short and the midday meal often consists of open sandwiches, so the hot meal of the day is eaten early, around 4 or 5 o'clock.

Norway extends more than 1,500 miles from north to south, so it comes as no surprise that diets vary widely. Shellfish are popular in the south, while whalemeat is considered a delicacy in the north. Crystal clear rivers provide a wealth of freshwater fish, including the noble salmon, and fish dishes are a specialty of Norwegian cuisine. Sheep and goats adapt more easily to the mountainous country than cattle, and game is always popular. Fish and meat are often preserved for consumption during the long, dark winters, especially in the Northern islands. Fish is dried in the ice cold winds, while mutton is salted or smoked first.

Norway was a poor country until the '50s, trading mostly in fish and timber and with little industrialization. Then, in 1968, came the discovery of oil in the North Sea, which reversed Norway's fortunes and in its wake brought Norwegians one of the world's highest standards of living. Today Norway is modern and highly industrialized, but nature still dominates vast areas of virgin land, allowing its people to enjoy both the benefits of a wealthy nation and the rare pleasures of the simple life.

*Children in national costume from Finmark –
the northernmost part of Scandinavia.*

DENMARK

The geographical position of the Danish peninsula and its numerous islands (there are about 450 of them) form a link between Europe and Scandinavia. In contrast to other Scandinavian countries, Denmark's landscape is flat or gently undulating, while the climate, tempered by the Gulf Stream, is warm in summer but wet and gray with little snow in winter.

In the country's 17,018 square miles live 5 million Danes a peace-loving people who take pride in their efficient, state-funded social welfare system and in their high standard of living. But it was not always so. Jylland (Jutland) was inhabited by nomadic hunters until, in AD500, a tribe from Sweden moved south. The tribe was known as "Danes." The land they moved to became Denmark.

The country's strategic position and Viking expansionism led to many struggles with England and Western Europe for control of the North Sea; with Norway and Sweden for the straits between Denmark and Norway; and with Germany, Poland, and Russia for the Baltic.

The Vikings were skilled and daring seafarers with swift, seaworthy ships – a big advantage in their many voyages and successful raids. They occupied much of England and Ireland, and continued south along the coast of France, on to Sicily, and as far as the Black Sea. To the north, their voyages took them to Iceland, Greenland, and Canada.

As Europe learned to defend its territories, Viking dominance receded. By the 18th century, Denmark had become a democracy, and its energies were turned toward cultural pursuits.

The principal islands of Denmark differ widely in character. The statue of the Little Mermaid is a well-known landmark in cosmopolitan Copenhagen on the island of

The famous Legoland town in Denmark.

Zealand. The capital's Tivoli Gardens is a bustling center of entertainment, and in the north of the island is Hamlet's Kronborg Castle. Fyn was the home of Hans Christian Andersen, and this island's rich farmlands have earned it a reputation as the granary of Denmark. Fruit comes from the orchards of Lolland and Falster, and here, too, amber is found and made into jewelry.

Many Stone Age monuments are found on the island of Mon, which is also distinguished by 12th- and 13th- century village churches, decorated with frescos depicting Biblical scenes.

Bornholm is Denmark's vacation island, 88 miles east of the mainland. Golden fields, prosperous farms, and forests mirror the Danish landscape in miniature, and old village inns provide warm hospitality.

Fish is the principal export of the Faroe Islands (there are 18 of them), which are also renowned for their knitwear.

Danes love good food, and need little encouragement to stop for coffee and a Danish pastry or a Danish open sandwich (smørrebrød) between meals. Local cooking combines wholesome country fare with the refinement of aristocratic culinary skills, which were themselves influenced by foreign lands, and French cuisine in particular.

Danes eat more meat than other Scandinavians. Home-produced pork, hams, and bacon are favorites. Small game, such as hare and pheasant, are also popular, and chicken is traditional on Sundays. Fish and Denmark's wide assortment of cheeses also feature very prominently on the menu.

Fertile, mild Denmark is Scandinavia's "land of milk and honey," where the scenery, culture, and food of north and south meet and mix to the benefit of all.

SWEDEN

Look at the map of Sweden and you begin to grasp the size of this vast Scandinavian country. Sweden stretches almost 1,000 miles from its barren, arctic northern tip to its fertile south. It is the fourth-largest country in Europe, but its population has remained relatively small (8.5 million) and thinly spread. It is a country of staggering contrasts, with vast forests covering 50 percent of the land, innumerable lakes, including two of the largest in Europe, desolate moorland, and rushing rivers. Although relatively flat or gently rolling for the most part, the land mass is broken by a mountain range in the northwest with peaks rising to more than 6,000 feet and the coastline is dotted with countless islands that make popular summer retreats.

Elk, reindeer, bear, and lynx roam the forests; lakes and rivers are a rich source of fish; while sea eagles and ospreys soar high in the sky.

The climate is one of harsh contrasts, with warm summers and long hours of daylight, earning the country its reputation as the land of the midnight sun, followed by bitterly cold, dark winters. Contrasts continue between Sweden's Viking past and its ultramodern cities; shops filled with the latest designs in goods and fashions highlight Sweden's regard for the traditional skills of woodcarving, weaving, and glass blowing. The music of the '40s and '50s is widely heard despite the international reputation of rock groups such as Abba, and sexual liberation is tempered by the high value placed on family life.

Traditional festivals have an important place in the Swedish calendar. Typical of the country's annual celebrations are the Feast of Valborg on April 30th, when bonfires are lit to mark the end of winter, and the Midsummer Day festivities, when Swedes decorate their homes with garlands of flowers, dance around maypoles, and stay up with the sun throughout the night. But perhaps the best-known festival, and one that is said to have its roots in pagan times, is that of the Day of Santa Lucia, Queen of Light, on December 13th. Young girls chosen to represent the saint wear a crown of candles in their hair (usually an electric substitute nowadays) and, accompanied by

A typical Swedish harbor, with wooden houses bordering the water's edge.

their handmaidens, they "reign" over the celebrations that mark the beginning of the Christmas season.

Preserving the natural heritage is also high on Sweden's list of priorities and, as a result, fish abound even in the waters of downtown Stockholm, and hares have adopted the parks of Malmö!

Stockholm is considered to be one of Europe's most beautiful capital cities. Built on fourteen islands, it is a city of green parks, handsome squares, and airy boulevards. It is also a city of contrasts, with ultramodern skyscrapers never more than a few minutes walk from medieval streets. Stockholm's efficient infrastructure of roads and railways make it possible for Stockholmers to live in the suburbs built in the pine forests, and by the lakesides around the capital. Sweden is rich in natural resources. In addition to a thriving industry in pulp, paper, and wood products (60 percent of which go to export), natural resources include uranium, iron ore, and other metals. Hydroelectric plants account for about 15 percent of energy supplies, and this cheap source of power has played a major part in Sweden's industrial development.

Swedish cooking is wholesome and tasty. The laden *smörgåsbord* table is perhaps the most widely known of their delicacies. Every housewife takes great pride in the preparation of this meal, which consists of a selection of delicacies served buffet style. The origin of the *smörgåsbord* is said to go back more than 200 years, when it was the traditional meal of country people.

Fish (fresh, smoked, or pickled) is a specialty, and herring is a particular favorite. In season, hunting is popular, adding elk, venison, hare, and all types of game to the cuisine. Autumn brings an exotic variety of mushrooms and fruits, such as blackberries, blueberries, and cranberries, with the country's rich dairy products forming the basis of excellent pastries and delicious creamy desserts.

Sweden is often described as a "rich" country, a fact reflected in the wealth of its natural resources, the abundance of its wildlife, and the quality of life enjoyed and carefully protected by its people.

FINLAND

A team of huskies pulling a sled over the
snowbound landscape of Finland.

The culture and the way of life of the people of Finland is unique – even in Scandinavia. The population is spread far and wide across the land, and their culture is closely linked to nature – not surprising since the forest is everywhere, even in the heart of the capital, Helsinki. The extensive moorlands and swamps of southern and central Finland are interspersed with forest and lakes, while the north gradually makes way to tundra, where moss and lichen replace fir trees and dense forest vegetation.

Finnish handicrafts are also very distinctive from those of other nordic nations. Utensils have been handmade for centuries, and carving skills are passed on from one generation to the next in isolated villages. The children begin to learn the craft at an early age, devoting much of their life to perfecting their skills.

Strictly speaking, Finns are not Scandinavian, and their native tongue is a link with their distant past. Their ancestors came from central Asia and moved north to settle on the swampy shores of the Gulf of Finland, displacing the Lapps, who moved farther north still, into Lapland.

Sweden and Russia fought over Finland for centuries and, after more than 600 years under Swedish rule and 100 under the czars of Russia, it is inevitable that Finland should bear traces of their two cultures.

One third of Finland lies north of the Arctic Circle, and although temperatures here can drop to –20°F in winter, the effect of the Gulf Stream makes it the warmest of the Scandinavian countries in summer, when temperatures are often over 68°F. The winter months (mid-November to February) are cold and dark. Summer is short, but very light – in the extreme north the sun doesn't set at all during June and July – and it is in this brief period that crops are grown.

Gratins and stews are popular in Finland, and a gratin of swede, a favorite vegetable, is a traditional Christmas Day dish. Breads range from flatbreads and crispbreads (mainly in the west and reflecting the influence of Sweden) to sour-dough rye (typical in the east and also found in Russia and central Europe). Fish stews are an economical way of utilizing the heat left over after baking. Thick gruels and porridges are popular, made from different grains and topped with berry purées or cream. The Finns produce their own version of the Swedish *smörgåsbord*, but their cuisine also reflects the borscht soup and meat kebabs of neighboring Russia.

Although the food of Finland reflects the influence of its neighbors, both east and west, it is based on the produce of its land. Finns see the fruits and wildlife of nature as a gift to be cherished. Their calm approach to life is a result of their love of the nature that surrounds them.

1

SOUPS

SUMMER VEGETABLE SOUP
KESAKEITTO

Made from summer vegetables picked at their absolute peak of freshness, this is a light, healthy soup. It is a favorite for a lunch or a late supper. The meal is often finished with small pancakes and jam.

SERVES 6–8

4 small carrots

1½ cups frozen peas

1 small cauliflower

2 new potatoes

½lb string beans

4 small radishes, halved

¼lb fresh spinach, washed

2 tsp salt

2 tbsp butter

2 tbsp plain flour

½ cup milk

1 egg yolk

¼ cup heavy cream

½lb small peeled shrimp

1 tsp white pepper

2 tbsp finely chopped fresh dill or parsley

Prepare and cut the vegetables into ¼-inch cubes, except for the peas and spinach. Place the cubed vegetables and peas in a saucepan, cover with cold water, and add the salt. Boil, uncovered, for 5 minutes, or until tender. Add the spinach, and cook for another 5 minutes. Strain the liquid into a bowl, and put the vegetables into another bowl.

Melt the butter, remove from the heat, and stir in the flour. Slowly add the hot vegetable stock, whisking all the time, then beat in the milk. Mix the egg yolk and cream in a small bowl. Whisk ⅔ cup of the hot soup into the egg mixture, spooning it in. Then whisk the warmed egg and cream mixture back into the soup.

Add the vegetables to the soup and reheat. Just before it boils, add the shrimp and simmer for 3–4 minutes. Season to taste. Serve with chopped dill or parsley.

BEER SOUP

ØLLEBRØD

SERVES 4–6

8 slices of pumpernickel

2½ cups dark malt beer
  or brown ale

1 cup water

grated rind and juice of 1 lemon

sugar, to taste

⅔ cup whipped cream

This very popular Danish soup, rarely tasted by foreigners, should be as thick as porridge. A sweet, dark, non-alcoholic malt beer is traditionally used.

Cut the bread into small pieces, and place in a deep dish. Pour the beer and water over the bread, and leave to soak for a minimum of 3 hours.

Transfer the mixture to a saucepan, and simmer over a low heat until it thickens to the desired consistency. Purée in a food processor at medium speed. Add the lemon rind and juice, and sweeten with sugar to taste. Return to the heat and bring to the boil. Serve hot with whipped cream.

FINE FISH SOUP

FIN FISKESUPPE

SERVES 4–6

2lb turbot or brill

4½ cups water

2 tsp salt

3–4 peppercorns

1 medium onion, sliced

1 carrot

1 leek

1 green pepper

1 small can pimento

¼ cup oil

1 tbsp butter

½ tsp curry powder

1 clove garlic, crushed

⅔–1 cup white wine

salt and pepper

All the flavor of fish and fresh vegetables, plus a tang of garlic and spices, makes this a fine soup.

Clean and fillet the fish. To make the stock, discard the gills, then put the fish head, skin, and bones in a saucepan with the water, salt, peppercorns, and onion. Bring to the boil, reduce the heat, and simmer the stock for about 30 minutes, then strain it. Cut the fish fillets into narrow pieces, and simmer in some of the fish stock for 5–10 minutes.

Prepare and cut the vegetables into fine strips. Cook in the oil and butter with the curry powder and garlic until all the vegetables are tender. Add the wine and boil for a few minutes. Add the fish stock, and simmer the soup until the vegetables are tender. Add the fish and heat through thoroughly. Season to taste.

NETTLE SOUP

NÄSSELSOPPA

SERVES 4–6

½lb fresh young nettles

salt and pepper

5 tbsp chopped fresh chives

2 tbsp butter

3 tbsp flour

5–6 cups beef stock

All that is needed for this first taste of spring is a plastic bag and a pair of gloves for picking those young, tender shoots while out on your spring walk. For color, add hard-boiled eggs, shrimp, and croûtons.

Rinse the nettles thoroughly in cold water. Boil them for about 15 minutes until tender in lightly salted water. Drain and finely chop the nettles with the chives.

 Melt the butter, add the flour, and cook for 2–3 minutes, stirring continuously. When golden brown, add the beef stock and boil for 10 minutes. Add the nettles and chives to the soup. Season with salt and pepper. If liked, serve with a poached egg or half a hard-boiled egg per person.

YELLOW PEA SOUP WITH PORK

GUL ÄRTSOPPA MED FLÄSK

SERVES 4–6

2 cups dried yellow peas

9 cups water

¾lb lightly smoked pork, soaked
  overnight

1 small onion or leek, chopped

½ tsp dried marjoram

salt and pepper

A wholesome soup and almost a meal in itself on a cold day. The smoky flavor of the meat combines well with the yellow peas, and marjoram adds piquancy.

Rinse and soak the peas in the cold water for 10 hours. Cook the peas in fresh water. Bring to the boil quickly, and remove any floating pea shells. Put the lid on, and repeat the process a few times until most of the floating shells are removed.

 Add the pork to the peas with the onion and marjoram. Cover and simmer for about 2 hours. Remove the pork, and cut into small pieces. Return the pork pieces to the soup. Season to taste. Serve hot with plenty of mustard.

CREME SAINT-GERMAIN

GRÖN SOPPA

SERVES 4–6

1 medium onion, sliced

1–2 tbsp butter or margarine

4½ cups veal or chicken stock

3 cups fresh peas or

   1 small can and 1 small packet

   frozen peas

1 tbsp flour

1–2 tbsp brandy or Madeira

salt and pepper

1 egg yolk

½ cup light cream

HORSERADISH CREAM

⅔ cup heavy cream

2–2½ tsp grated horseradish

CHEESE CROÛTONS

1¾ cups flour

1½ cups Swiss cheese, grated

pinch of salt

½ cup butter or margarine

2 tbsp ice-cold water

1 egg for glazing

A classic soup with a mild, delicate flavor, which gets a kick from the horseradish cream.

Fry the onion in a little of the butter or margarine, without browning. Pour in the stock and add the peas. Boil the mixture for 15 minutes. Blend in a food processor, then strain.

Melt 1 tbsp butter or margarine and stir in the flour. Cook for 2–3 minutes, stirring. Gradually add the strained soup, and stir in the brandy or wine and season to taste.

Whisk together the egg yolk and cream in a soup terrine, and pour in the soup, stirring vigorously. Serve the soup in heated bowls, garnished with a swirl of horseradish cream and cheese croûtons. To make the horseradish cream, simply mix the cream and grated horseradish together.

For the croûtons, mix the flour, cheese, and salt together. Crumble the margarine or butter into the mixture. Add the water and quickly mix the pastry together into a ball. Let the pastry rest in a cool place for 30 minutes.

Preheat the oven to 475°F. Roll out the pastry to a thickness of ⅛ inch, and cut out croûtons. Brush with beaten egg, and place on a baking sheet. Bake until golden. Serve warm.

A herd of reindeer graze for scraps of edible matter in the snow.

SWEDE SOUP

KÅLROTSUPPE

SERVES 4–6

1 swede

6¼ cups beef stock

1 tbsp butter

1 tbsp flour

½ cup light cream

pinch of salt

pepper

1 tbsp chopped fresh parsley

A good winter soup that is easy to prepare and economical. Adding a touch of cream gives it a silky-smooth texture.

Peel and cut the swede into slices. Boil it in the beef stock for about 25 minutes, until tender. Remove and press through a sieve or mash finely, reserving the stock.

Melt the butter in a saucepan, and mix in the flour. Cook for 2–3 minutes, stirring. Add the stock and swede pulp. Simmer for 10 minutes. Whip the cream in a tureen. Add the soup, stirring slowly. Season, then sprinkle with chopped parsley.

GOOSE GIBLET SOUP

KRAASESUPPE

SERVES 4–6

gizzard, wings, neck, feet, and
   heart of a goose

3¾ cups water

4 leeks

4 carrots

2 stalks of celery

2 tsp salt

4 peppercorns

6 medium tart apples

1½ cups prunes, pitted

¼ cup sugar

1½ cups water

½ cup butter

½ cup flour

6¼ cups giblet stock and prune
   and apple juice, mixed

The Danes are very fond of goose, and thick, nourishing soups. Since they are also very thrifty, the leftovers of a goose are used to make many other meals, as well.

Clean the gizzard, and peel off the thick membrane. Cut the wings in half, and cut the neck into a few pieces. Remove the skin and claws from the feet. Wash the heart. Place all the giblets in a large saucepan with cold water, and bring to the boil. Prepare and cut the leeks, carrots, and celery into large pieces, and add to the giblets. Season with salt and peppercorns. Cover and simmer for about 2½ hours.

Peel, core, and slice the apples, and combine with the prunes, sugar, and water. Boil the fruit until tender. Drain and discard the fruit, saving the liquid.

Drain the meat, reserving the stock. Melt the butter, add the flour, and cook for 2–3 minutes, stirring. Gradually stir in the fruit liquid and stock from the meat. When thickened, return to the pan and cook over a low heat for 10 minutes. Serve with dumplings (page 61).

2

APPETIZERS AND SNACKS

SALMON MOUSSE

LAX MOUSSE

SERVES 4

1¼lb cooked salmon, boned

2½ tbsp lemon juice

1 tsp salt

cayenne pepper

gelatine

½ cup hot salmon liquid
  or water

3 tbsp mayonnaise

3 tbsp dill, finely chopped

⅔ cup heavy cream, whipped

asparagus tips, hard-boiled egg
  quarters, lemon slices, and
  sprigs of dill, to garnish

Delicious summer starter and so pretty, too. No need to panic before a dinner party either – the mousse can be prepared in advance and turned out just before serving. Individual molds make an attractive presentation for a very special occasion.

Flake the salmon with a fork. Mix in the lemon juice, salt, and a little cayenne pepper. Dissolve the gelatine in the hot salmon liquid or water. Leave to cool. Mix with the flaked salmon. Add the mayonnaise, dill, and whipped cream.

Rinse a 10-inch mold in cold water. Spoon the mousse into the mold, or into smaller individual molds. Refrigerate until set. Turn out and garnish with asparagus tips, hard-boiled egg quarters, lemon slices, and dill sprigs.

◄ *Salmon mousse*

LUMPFISH ROE ON TOAST

LÖJROMS TOAST

SERVES 4

4 slices of brown bread (round,
  if available)

3–4 tbsp butter

½lb fresh or frozen peeled shrimp,
  thawed

½ cup mayonnaise

a little tomato paste and
  Worcestershire sauce

4 slices of lemon

6-oz can lumpfish roe or bleak roe

dill, to garnish

A really easy and delicious starter for a party, this dish was inspired by Hamburger Börs, a Stockholm restaurant with a great reputation.

Cut out round shapes from the 4 slices of bread, using a large glass or a cup as a guide. Fry the bread in the butter on both sides, then leave to cool.

Peel and chop the shrimp, and mix with the mayonnaise. Color and flavor with some tomato paste and Worcestershire sauce. Spread the mixture on the fried bread, placing a slice of lemon on top. Place the bleak roe or lumpfish roe on top of the lemon. Garnish with dill. Serve this delicious toast freshly made.

GLASS BLOWERS' HERRING

LASIMESTARIN SILLI

SERVES 4–6

4 medium herrings

3 medium red onions, sliced

2 carrots, sliced

MARINADE

1¼ cups pickling vinegar

1¼ cups sugar

2½ cups water

20 whole allspice

20 white peppercorns

4 bay leaves

Finns spend much of their time outdoors, hence their love of fresh fish. These tasty, spicy herrings are at their best when they have been marinated for a few days.

Gut and clean the herrings, then soak in cold water overnight. Drain and dry the herrings. Cut across in 1½–2-inch thick slices.

For the marinade, mix the vinegar, sugar, water, allspice, white peppercorns, and bay leaves. Bring to the boil, then allow to cool at room temperature.

Put the herrings and vegetables in layers in a glass jar. Pour in enough marinade to cover completely. Refrigerate for at least 24 hours before serving. Serve with boiled new potatoes and brown bread.

Glass blowers' herring ▶

HOMEMADE CHEESE

KOTIJUUSTO

SERVES 4–6

3 eggs

5 cups buttermilk

1 gallon plus 1½ cups milk

salt

chopped fresh parsley, to garnish

Every community has their own design of mold used for these simple cheeses, which are frequently served as a starter on a buffet table.

Whip the eggs and buttermilk until fluffy. Bring the milk to the boil, add the egg mixture, and beat well. Switch off the heat and leave the mixture on the stove to cool slowly. (Liquid will form on the top, and the cheese will settle on the bottom.)

Line a strainer or cheese mold with cheesecloth. Remove the cheese with a slotted spoon and put it into the lined strainer, sprinkling a little salt in between the layers. Cover with a plate as a weight, and refrigerate for 12 hours. Turn out the cheese onto a serving dish, and garnish with chopped parsley.

OPEN SANDWICHES

SMØRREBRØD

The open sandwich is the Danish national dish, and is enjoyed by everybody. It is said to have been popular with the upper classes as early as the 18th century. The open sandwich is a colorful meal in itself, and is eaten with a knife and fork. Cut into quarters, it can be served as a delightful hors d'oeuvre for parties and special occasions.

Use dark rye bread for open sandwiches; however, if you wish to use white bread, toast it first. The following ideas are suggestions for open sandwiches using all sorts of ingredients.

EGGS AND HERRING

 AEGS OG SILD

Spread slices of hard-boiled egg on buttered bread. Place one or more boned herrings lengthwise on the egg. Garnish with cress.

SMOKED SALMON AND SCRAMBLED EGG

ROGET LAKS OG RORAG

Place a piece of smoked salmon on buttered bread. On top of that, diagonally across the bread, spoon a strip of cold scrambled egg. Garnish with finely chopped dill.

ROAST BEEF AND FRIED EGG

BØF MED SPEJLAEG

Place tender slices of cold roast beef on buttered bread. Fry onions until golden and crisp and spread on the slices of beef. Top with a fried egg, and serve before the egg cools.

Note: Danish eggs are always served sunny side up!

THE HANS ANDERSEN SANDWICH

H.C. ANDERSEN SANDWICH

Butter a piece of bread, and put two rows of crisp bacon on top. Spread liver pâté across one row of bacon, and place tomato slices across the other. Top the tomato with horseradish and a strip of jellied consommé.

COLD ROAST PORK

FLAESKESTEG

Spread thin slices of roast pork on buttered bread. Garnish with crisp pieces of rind (crackling), slices of jellied consommé, cucumber or pickled gherkin, and beet or red cabbage.

FOR VEGETARIANS

ITALIAN SALAD

ITALIENSK SALAT

Mix together cooked chopped carrots, finely cut asparagus, peas, and mayonnaise. Place a lettuce leaf on buttered bread, and arrange a thick layer of the Italian salad on top. Garnish with tomato slices and cress. If you are using homemade mayonnaise, add a few drops of tarragon vinegar to the vegetables.

TOMATO WITH RAW ONION

TOMAT MED RAA LOG

Place several slices of tomato on buttered bread. Put a pile of finely chopped raw onion in the center.

APPETITE SANDWICH

APTITSMÖRGÅS

SERVES 4

4 slices of white or brown bread

1 large onion, finely chopped

1 scant tbsp butter

1 can anchovy fillets

1 tbsp chili sauce

2 tbsp chopped fresh parsley

2 tbsp chopped fresh dill

4 egg yolks

These sandwiches are bound to satisfy most appetites. They are spicy, tasty, and full of goodness – a real meal on a slice.

Cut out round shapes from the 4 slices of bread, using a glass or a cup as a guide. Toast the bread. Fry the onion in the butter until soft and golden. Cut the anchovy fillets into small pieces, and mix with the onion. Add the chili sauce, parsley, and dill, then quickly fry together.

Divide the mixture between the toasted bread slices. Make a hollow for the egg yolks, then place one yolk on each portion. Serve immediately while piping hot.

DANISH CHEESE MOUSSE

DANSK OSTEMOUSSE

SERVES 6–8

4oz Samsoe cheese

4oz Danish blue cheese

1¼ cups heavy cream

¼ cup walnuts, chopped

1 tbsp aspic jelly powder

2 tbsp water

2 egg whites

1–2 tsp mustard

1 tsp celery salt (optional)

pepper

sprigs of parsley and candied
   cherries, to garnish

Denmark is one of the biggest exporters of cheese in the world. Samsoe cheese takes its name from the Danish island of Samsoe. The flavor resembles that of Cheddar. Danish blue has a pleasant, sharp flavor.

Grate both cheeses into a large bowl. Whip the cream until light and fluffy, but not stiff. Stir in the chopped walnuts, then add the mixture to the cheese. Mix the aspic powder and water in a small bowl. Put the bowl in a saucepan of hot water and leave to stand until the powder has dissolved. Leave to cool. Whisk the egg whites until stiff, and fold them into the cheese mixture. Season with mustard, celery salt, if using, and pepper. Fold the aspic into the mixture.

Pour the mixture into a 1lb container or mold of your choice. Leave to set in a cool place. Turn out the mousse when required, and garnish with sprigs of parsley and candied cherries. Serve on toast or crackers.

Danish cheese mousse ▶

BLINIS

BLINIES

SERVES 4–6

1 oz packet fresh yeast

⅔ cup tepid water

¼ cup light cream

1¼ cups flour

2½ cups buckwheat flour

1¾ cups hot milk

3 tbsp melted butter

1 tsp salt

2 eggs, separated

These are classic Russian buckwheat pancakes served with fresh roe, which is seasonal. The finest roe is burbot, which is popular at Christmastime.

Dissolve the yeast in the tepid water. Add the cream and beat in the flours. Leave the batter to stand for 8–12 hours.

Add the hot milk, melted butter, and salt, and whisk. Add the egg yolks to the batter, whisking gently. Whisk the egg whites until stiff, and fold into the batter just before frying.

Fry the pancakes gently in a frying pan in the remaining butter for 2–3 minutes on each side. Serve hot with fresh roe, chopped raw onions, freshly ground pepper, and sour cream.

LIVER PÂTÉ

MAKSAPASTEIJA

SERVES 4-6

1½ cup light cream

½ cup fresh breadcrumbs

2 medium onions, finely chopped

2 tbsp butter

1 lb finely chopped liver (ask for the liver to be ground twice)

4 tbsp potato flour

1 tbsp sugar

3 tbsp salt

1 tbsp ground ginger

1 tbsp white pepper

2 eggs, lightly beaten

thin slices of belly of pork or bacon

Frequently served as part of the Christmas Eve feast, this liver pâté can be served hot or cold. For a treat, serve with loganberry or cranberry jam or jelly.

Mix the cream and breadcrumbs, then leave to swell. Preheat the oven to 475°F. Fry the onions in the butter until soft. Leave to cool.

Mix the liver and the rest of the ingredients, except the slices of belly pork, and blend thoroughly. Line a baking dish with the belly of pork. Pour the mixture into the baking dish, and cover tightly with foil. Put the dish into a roasting pan of water. Bake for about 2 hours. Refrigerate before serving.

Christmas is a time of special celebration in all Scandinavian countries.

FILLED BREAD LOAF AU GRATIN

GRATINERAD LANDGÅNG

SERVES 4–6

1 small white or brown loaf

¼ lb smoked sausage

2oz cheese

2 tomatoes

¼ cup softened butter

1 medium onion, chopped

chopped fresh parsley

Gratinerad Landgång makes an unusual but very tasty snack.

Preheat the oven to 475°F. Slice the loaf, but do not cut right through to the bottom. Place the bread on a large piece of foil. Cut the smoked sausage, cheese, and tomatoes into cubes. Mix into the butter with the onion and parsley.

Spread the mixture between the slices of bread. Fold up the foil all around the bread. Bake for 15 minutes.

FISH AND SHELLFISH

Sandwichgateau with salmon and shellfish

Boiled cod

Parsley sauce

Fish balls

Bornholm omelet

Fish pie

Marinated salmon

Dill and mustard sauce

Tasty fish fillets

Shrimp and roe in a bread basket

Curried fish

Oven-roasted pike

Fried Baltic herring with a taste of France

Matjes herring with tomatoes and olives

Fish balls with tomatoes, onion, and celery

Fish au gratin

Shrimp in dill cream

Smoked salmon with filling

Herring with leek and lemon

Fresh salted salmon

Weiner Christiansen's Singapore eel

SANDWICHGATEAU WITH SALMON AND SHELLFISH

SMÖRGÅSTÅRTA

SERVES 4–6

1 round or oblong white or brown loaf, cut into ½-inch thick slices

FILLING

6 hard-boiled eggs, chopped

2 x 6oz cans crab meat

¼lb smoked salmon

½ cup sour cream or Greek yogurt

½ cup mayonnaise

3 tbsp finely chopped fresh chives

3 tbsp finely chopped fresh dill

salt and pepper

This delicious sandwichgâteau is filled and covered with smoked salmon and shellfish.

Mix all the ingredients for the filling, then divide it between the layers of bread.

Mix the mayonnaise with the sour cream or yogurt. Do not stir too much. Spread the mixture on top and around the side of the loaf for a smooth finish. Garnish with shrimp, folded salmon, roe, and slices of cucumber and lemon. Cut into portions with a very sharp knife. Serve with a green salad.

GARNISH

½ cup mayonnaise

½ cup sour cream or Greek yogurt

1 lb shrimp

¼–½ lb smoked salmon

small (2–3oz) jar lumpfish or bleak roe

½ fresh cucumber, sliced

slices of lemon

◄ *Sandwichgateau with salmon and shellfish*

BOILED COD

KOGT TORSK

SERVES 4–6

6 cups cod

scant 2 tbsp salt

2 tbsp light malt vinegar

5 cups water

chopped fresh parsley, to garnish

It is claimed that Danish fish is so good that you have to go all the way to California to find its equal. This dish is often served on New Year's Eve.

Cut the fish into large pieces. Sprinkle with half of the salt, leave for 10–15 minutes, then rinse the fish thoroughly and place in a saucepan. Add the rest of the salt, the vinegar, and the water. Cover and bring the fish gently to the boil. Switch off the heat, and leave the fish to stand for about 10 minutes.

Drain the fish. Garnish with chopped parsley. Serve with boiled potatoes, chopped hard-boiled eggs, and grated horseradish.

PARSLEY SAUCE

PERSILLESAUS

SERVES 4–6

2 tbsp butter

¼ cup flour

2¼ cups warm fish stock
   or bouillon

2 tbsp finely chopped fresh parsley

salt and pepper

This delicious and simple sauce makes an excellent accompaniment to many plain fish dishes, including Fish Balls.

Melt the butter in a pan, add the flour, and cook for 2–3 minutes, stirring continuously. Slowly pour in the warm fish stock, stirring all the time. Boil for 10 minutes. Add the parsely and season to taste. Serve with the fish balls (see below).

FISH BALLS

FISKE FARSE

SERVES 4–6

2¾lb fresh fish, finely chopped

salt and white pepper

4½ cups fish stock

The delicate flavor of fish is carefully preserved by this gentle way of cooking. The parsley sauce, using fish stock, adds to the flavor of the dish.

Season the chopped fish with salt and white pepper. Shape into small, round balls. Heat the fish stock in a pan. Put the fish balls into the hot fish stock and simmer gently for 3–5 minutes, until tender. Serve the fish balls with Parsley Sauce (see above), boiled potatoes, green peas, and salad.

BORNHOLM OMELET

BORNHOLM AEGGEKAGE

SERVES 4–6

6 eggs

¾ cup milk or light cream

1 tsp salt

¼ cup butter

3 small smoked herrings, boned

15–20 radishes

1 head of lettuce

2 tbsp chopped fresh chives

Bornholm is the little paradise island in the Baltic Sea, famous for its unique cliffs, sandy beaches, woods, picturesque little towns, and fresh or smoked herring. This unusual omelet has an excellent combination of flavors.

Beat the eggs, milk, and salt together. Melt the butter in a frying pan and add the egg mixture. Cook to the desired consistency.

Slice the herrings, radishes, lettuce, and chives. Sprinkle on top of the omelet.

Bornholm omelet ▶

FISH PIE

PATAKUKKO

SERVES 4–6

2lb small perch or vendace

10oz fatty pork, cut
   into strips

1½–2 tbsp salt

DOUGH

1¾ cups rye flour

⅓ cup water

⅓ cup white flour

1 tsp salt

This fish pie is a typical dish from Karelia, in Finland, and can easily be carried around. As it is so portable, try it in the children's lunch box or on picnics.

Clean the fish, and sprinkle with salt. Leave the fish to stand in the refrigerator for a few hours or overnight to allow the salt to soak in. Line a baking dish with strips of the pork. Place the fish in the baking dish and add a drop of water.

Preheat the oven to 325°F. Mix together the rye flour, water, white flour, and salt to make the dough. Knead it well on a floured board. Roll out the dough and use to cover the fish in the baking dish. Bake for 2–3 hours until golden.

MARINATED SALMON

GRAVAD LAX

SERVES 4–6

2–3lb fresh salmon (middle cut)

¼ cup salt

⅓ cup sugar

plenty of fresh dill

1½ tbsp crushed whole white
   peppercorns

Prepare your own Gravad lax with salmon, trout, or mackerel. You will be surprised how easy it is, and how delicious. The dill and mustard sauce is a perfect accompaniment.

Ask for the salmon to be cut into fillets, and have the central bone removed. Remove any remaining small bones. Mix the salt and sugar together.

Take a shallow dish and sprinkle with half of the dill. Place one of the salmon fillets on the dill, skin side down. Rub half the mixture of salt and sugar into the salmon. Sprinkle with crushed white peppercorns and half the remaining dill. Repeat the process on the other side of salmon and sandwich together, skin side up. Cover with foil.

Refrigerate for 3 days, turning the salmon every 24 hours. To serve, scrape off the seasoning and cut in slices, discarding the skin. Serve with Dill and Mustard Sauce (page 40).

◄ *Marinated salmon*

DILL AND MUSTARD SAUCE

GRAVLAX SÅS

SERVES 4–6

1 tbsp sugar

2 tbsp malt vinegar

2 tbsp mild mustard

finely chopped fresh dill

7 tbsp oil

salt and white pepper

As well as accompanying Gravad Lax, this sauce can also be served with other types of fish.

Mix the sugar, vinegar, mustard, and dill together. Pour the oil slowly into the mixture, stirring thoroughly. Season with salt and white pepper. Serve with Gravad Lax (page 39).

TASTY FISH FILLETS

FISKEFILETER MED SMAK

SERVES 4–6

6 small tomatoes

1 tsp salt

1 tsp pepper

juice of ½ lemon

½ cup dry white wine

1 tbsp finely chopped fresh
   parsley

2 tsp fresh tarragon

1½lb fish fillets, such as plaice or
   whiting

2 tbsp finely chopped onion

SAUCE

½lb fresh or canned
   button mushrooms, sliced

⅓ cup butter

2 tbsp plain flour

1 cup fish stock

2 egg yolks

½ cup light cream

This recipe gives white fish a colorful new look. Wrapped around a tomato and served on a creamy mushroom sauce, the fillets taste as good as they look.

Scald the tomatoes, and sprinkle them with salt and pepper. Mix the lemon juice with the wine, parsley, and tarragon. Place the fish fillets in the marinade, sprinkle with salt and pepper, then leave to soak for about 30 minutes.

Preheat the oven to 400°F. Wrap a fish fillet around each tomato. Sprinkle the finely chopped onion in the base of a buttered, ovenproof dish. Place the fish and tomato rolls side by side in the dish, then pour the marinade over them. Cover the dish with foil, and bake for about 20 minutes.

For the sauce, brown the mushroom slices lightly in the butter. Sprinkle in the flour and cook for 2–3 minutes, then stir in the fish stock and bring to the boil. Mix the egg yolks into the cream. Stir into the sauce; do not boil. Add salt and pepper to taste. Pour some of the sauce into a serving dish, and place the fish rolls on top. Serve the remaining sauce together with boiled rice.

Tasty fish fillets ▶

SHRIMP AND ROE IN A BREAD BASKET

RÄKOR OCH LÖJROM I TUNNBRÖDSKORG

SERVES 4

¼lb peeled fresh shrimp

4 tbsp mayonnaise

Italian seasoning

1 bunch of chopped dill

4 slices of thin, unleavened bread,
  such as fine matzos

½ iceberg lettuce, chopped

4oz jar lumpfish or bleak roe

1 lemon, cut into wedges

This dish is easy to make and is much appreciated, as it is colorful and very attractively presented.

Finely chop the shrimp. Mix with the mayonnaise, and sprinkle lightly with Italian seasoning. Add the dill, saving some for garnishing.

To make the bread basket, moisten each piece of bread with water and quickly turn over in a hot, dry frying pan. Lift up the bread slice, which is now pliable, and place over an inverted glass. Carefully press the bread against glass all around to form a basket. (When the bread has cooled it will be firm, and the basket will be ready.)

One third fill the basket with chopped iceberg lettuce. Add the shrimp mixture. Shape the roe with a dessertspoon and place on top. Garnish with the remaining dill and lemon wedges.

CURRIED FISH

FISK MED CURRY

SERVES 4–6

1¼ cups water

1 cup dry white wine

1 small leek or onion, sliced

5 white peppercorns

1½ tsp salt

1–1¼lb white fish fillets

boiled long grain rice, to serve

almonds or salted peanuts fried
  in oil, to garnish

This curry sauce is equally good with chicken. Fried almonds add a delicious touch. Lettuce dressed with lemon vinaigrette is a good accompaniment.

Mix the water, wine, leek or onion, peppercorns, and salt in a pan. Bring to the boil, cover, and simmer for 10 minutes.

Rinse the fish fillets, fold them double, and place in a wide saucepan. Strain the liquid and pour onto the fish. Simmer for 6–8 minutes.

For the sauce, melt the butter, add the curry powder and flour, and heat without browning. Add the fish stock gradually, stirring, and simmer for a few minutes. Remove from the heat, and whisk in the egg yolk with the cream. Season.

Place the fish on a bed of boiled rice, and pour over some of the sauce. Serve the rest separately. Garnish with fried almonds or salted peanuts.

CURRY SAUCE

2 tbsp butter

1½ tsp curry powder

2 tbsp flour

1¼ cups strained fish stock

1 egg yolk

½–1 cup light cream

salt and pepper

OVEN-ROASTED PIKE

UGNSBAKAD GÄDDA

SERVES 4–6

2lb pike

2 tsp salt

1 egg, beaten

breadcrumbs for coating

1 tsp ground white pepper

4–6 anchovy fillets

½ cup butter, melted

3 cups (½lb)cheese, grated,
preferably Cheddar or Edam

Though a somewhat undervalued fish in the States, pike is popular in Sweden. It has a delicious, unusual flavor, that is well worth exploring.

Preheat the oven to 400°F. Scale the fish, leave the head on for flavor, but cut off the fins. Rinse and dry. Sprinkle with a little salt and leave for 5 minutes. Turn the fish in the beaten egg, then coat in breadcrumbs mixed with a little white pepper. Arrange the anchovy fillets on top of the fish.

Wrap in foil and bake for 20–30 minutes. Baste with melted butter a few times. Sprinkle with the grated cheese 5 minutes before the end of the cooking time. Serve with steamed vegetables of your choice and boiled potatoes.

FRIED BALTIC HERRING WITH A TASTE OF FRANCE

STEKT STRÖMMING MED FRANSK DOFT

SERVES 4

2lb whole herring or 1¼lb filleted
Baltic herring

1 tsp salt

7 tbsp breadcrumbs

2 cloves garlic, crushed

½ tsp salt

3 tbsp chopped fresh parsley

2 tbsp chopped fresh thyme and
rosemary

2 tbsp olive oil

Olive oil, garlic, and herbs add a French flavor to this easy and popular herring dish. Fresh sardines may be used instead.

Preheat the oven to 425°F. Clean and fillet the fish. Sprinkle the flesh side with salt, and fold with the skin outward. Place the fillets in rows in a greased ovenproof dish.

Mix the breadcrumbs, garlic, salt, herbs, and olive oil together. Sprinkle the mixture over the herrings. Bake for 20 minutes.

MATJES HERRING
WITH TOMATOES AND OLIVES

TOMATSILL

SERVES 4

2 Matjes herring fillets, canned
   in brine

4–6 shallots or small pickling
   onions

12–14 olives with pimento

MARINADE

¾ cup tomato catsup

1 tbsp pickling vinegar

2 tbsp sugar

pinch of salt

1 tsp crushed white pepper

3 tbsp oil

A traditional recipe for herrings in brine with the flavors imparted by the marinade. The Matjes are a perfect contrast to plain new potatoes.

Slice the herring into 2-inch strips. Slice the shallots into fine rings. Layer the herring, shallots, and olives in a glass jar.

   For the marinade, mix the catsup, pickling vinegar, sugar, salt, and pepper together. Stir and add the oil slowly. Pour the marinade over the herring to cover, and leave in the refrigerator for a few hours before serving. Served with new potatoes and brown bread.

Matjes herring with tomatoes and olives ▶

FISH BALLS WITH TOMATOES,
ONION, AND CELERY

FISKEBOLLER GRYTE

SERVES 4

1½lb fish balls in stock, cooked,
   see page 36

2 tbsp chopped onion

4 tbsp chopped celery

2 tbsp butter

10oz can tomatoes

3 cups frozen peas

salt and white pepper

Tasty and different, this fish ball stew is a typical example of the many Norwegian ways of preparing the abundance of fish in their waters.

Allow the fish balls to drain from the stock. Fry the onion and celery in the butter for a few minutes. Pour in the tomatoes together with their liquid, then add the peas. Simmer gently until the onion and celery are soft. Add the fish balls, and gently heat through. Season to taste. Serve with boiled potatoes or rice.

FISH AU GRATIN

FISKEGRATENG

SERVES 4–6

⅓ cup butter

¾ cup flour

1¾ cups milk

3 eggs, separated

½ tsp grated nutmeg

1–1½lb boiled white fish, such as
     cod, haddock, or coley,
     chopped

salt and pepper

1 tbsp breadcrumbs

melted butter, to serve

A tasty gratin of white fish with a hint of nutmeg. The addition of egg yolks adds a rich flavor and whipped egg whites make the dish delightfully light.

Preheat the oven to 325°F. Melt the butter in a saucepan and add the flour. Cook for 2–3 minutes, stirring continuously. Add the milk gradually, and bring to the boil. Leave to cool. Stir in the egg yolks, nutmeg, chopped fish, salt, and pepper. Finally, whisk the egg whites and fold in.

Place the fish mixture in a greased ovenproof dish, and sprinkle with the breadcrumbs. Bake for about 1 hour. Serve with melted butter.

SHRIMP IN DILL CREAM

RÄKOR MED DILLGRÄDDE

SERVES 4

1lb peeled shrimp

1½ cups finely chopped dill

1¼ cups whipping cream

gelatine

2 tbsp sherry

salt and white pepper

finely chopped fresh dill

1 cucumber, sliced

1 lettuce

4oz jar lumpfish roe

It is always an advantage when food can be prepared in advance for a dinner party. This dish can be served as a starter or for lunch.

Place the shrimp in a bowl, and add the finely chopped dill. Pour in the cream, and place in the refrigerator for a couple of hours.

Dissolve the gelatine in warm water. Drain the shrimp from the cream, and whisk the cream into the gelatine. Add the sherry and seasoning to taste. Add the shrimp to the cream. Pour the mixture into a chilled ring mold and keep in the refrigerator for 5–6 hours, until set.

Turn out the molded shrimp ring onto a serving plate. Sprinkle finely chopped dill on top. Garnish with cucumber slices, lettuce leaves, and lumpfish roe.

◄ *Shrimp in dill cream*

SMOKED SALMON WITH FILLING
RÖKT LAXROS

SERVES 4

4–8 lettuce leaves

⅔ cup whipping cream

1 tbsp lemon juice

salt and white pepper

3–4 tsp creamed horseradish

¾lb fresh shrimp, peeled; or 6oz
    peeled shrimp

8 thin slices of smoked salmon

fresh dill, to garnish

Smoked salmon is delicious served by itself, but filled with shrimp and horseradish it is mouth-watering.

Rinse the lettuce leaves and pat dry. Arrange them on a serving plate. Whip the cream, adding the lemon juice, and season to taste. Fold in the creamed horseradish. Add the shrimp, saving a few for the garnish.

Spread the shrimp mixture onto the salmon slices. Roll them into "roses," and place on top of the lettuce leaves. Garnish the "roses" with shrimp and fresh dill.

Smoked salmon with filling ▶

HERRING WITH LEEK AND LEMON
SILL MED PURJOLÖK OCH CITRON

SERVES 4–6

2 salt herrings (4 fillets)

1 leek, cleaned and sliced

1 small bunch of dill, coarsely
    chopped

MARINADE

juice of 2 lemons

2 tbsp pickling vinegar

1 cup water

¾ cup sugar

½ tsp whole allspice

½ tsp white peppercorns

1 bay leaf

The leek and lemon juice add a tangy flavor to the herring – one of the many ways of serving this bountiful fish from the northern waters.

Fillet the salt herrings, and soak them in water overnight. Mix all the ingredients for the marinade in a saucepan and bring to the boil. Leave to cool.

Slice the herrings into 1-inch strips. Layer in a glass jar with the sliced leek and dill. When the marinade is cold, pour over enough liquid to cover the herrings. Leave in the refrigerator for 24 hours before serving. Serve with boiled new potatoes.

FRESH SALTED SALMON

TOURESUOLATTU LOHI

SERVES 4–6

1 piece middle-cut salmon, about 3½lb

⅔ cup salt

1 tbsp sugar

3–4 tbsp coarse white pepper

fresh dill

MUSTARD DRESSING

3 tbsp coarse grain mustard

2 tbsp sugar

4 tbsp white wine vinegar

¾ cup olive oil

chopped fresh dill

A traditional delicacy for the Christmas table that is easy to prepare. To reach its full flavor, the Finns leave the salmon outside in the snow for 2–3 days. This dish does not need any dressing but, if preferred, serve with a coarse mustard dressing.

Fillet the salmon, leaving the skin on. Wipe the salmon carefully with paper towels (do not rinse). Sprinkle half the salt into a suitable sized dish and place one fillet, skin side down, on top. Sprinkle the sugar and coarse white pepper over both fillets then place the second fillet, skin side up, on top of the first. Sprinkle the dill and remaining salt over the salmon.

Cover the dish with foil, and put a small weight on top. Keep in a cool place for 1–3 days. To serve, scrape off all the seasoning and cut the fillets into diagonal slices.

If liked, serve with mustard dressing. Mix together the mustard, sugar, and vinegar. Add the oil slowly, stirring continuously. Add plenty of chopped fresh dill.

WEINER CHRISTIANSEN'S SINGAPORE EEL

SINGAPORE AEL

SERVES 4–6

3lb fresh eel, skinned

¼ cup butter

2 tbsp mild curry powder

8–10 small carrots, sliced

4 stalks of celery, sliced

½lb small mushrooms

1 x 14oz can of tomatoes

1 tsp salt

¼ tsp ground black pepper

¼ cup fish stock or water

1 cup dry white wine

This superb Danish dish is served in many famous restaurants in Copenhagen. It can also be made with shrimp.

Cut the eel into 1½-inch pieces. Heat the butter, stir in the curry powder, and cook over a medium heat for 2 minutes, stirring constantly. Add all the vegetables. After 2 minutes, add the eel, season, then stir in the stock and wine. Cover and simmer over a low heat for 20 minutes, stirring occasionally. Serve with rice.

MEAT, POULTRY, AND GAME

Pork with apples

Raw spiced fillet of beef with spicy sauce

Potato dumplings stuffed with bacon

Ptarmigan (grouse)

Meat loaf en croûte

Braised venison

Meat cakes

Dumplings

Robertos veal roulades

Karelian stew

Meatballs

Sweetbreads with garlic mayonnaise

Gourmet lamb

Ryypy

Venison with goat's cheese

Summer omelet with sausages

Palace steak

Lamb and cabbage stew

Swedish hash

Meat patties

Easter chicken casserole

Liver and rice casserole

Roast goose

Grouse with cream sauce

Easter veal

Creamed sweetbreads

Fillet of veal à la Oscar

Pigs' feet

PORK WITH APPLES

SVINEKØD MED
AEBLE

Denmark's favorite meat is pork. The pig in one way or another is the Danes' key export. They have numerous ways of preparing pork, but it would be hard to find a more delicious version than this particular dish.

SERVES 4

1lb package bacon slices

2lb red eating apples

¼ cup sugar

Fry the bacon gently and pour off any excess fat into a dish during frying. This will make the bacon nice and crispy. Remove the bacon and keep warm.

Wash, core and slice the apples, but do not peel them. Fry the apple slices in a little of the bacon fat until soft. Sprinkle a little sugar over the apples. Place the fried apples and warm bacon slices in a serving dish. Serve with fried onions or leftovers. This recipe can be used as a topping for open sandwiches.

RAW SPICED FILLET OF BEEF
WITH SPICY SAUCE
GRAVAD OXFILE (MED SENAPSÅS)

SERVES 4

1lb piece fillet
  of beef
cress, chopped

MARINADE

¼ cup Madeira
2 tbsp red wine
1 tbsp olive oil
2 tbsp each of crushed white
  peppercorns and allspice
  (or black pepper)
1–2 tsp grated horseradish
plenty of chopped chives
  or leeks
chopped fresh parsley

SPICY SAUCE

3 tbsp unsweetened mustard
½ tsp sugar
½ tsp salt
1 egg yolk
generous ½ cup oil

Often simply served with an undressed green salad and bread.
Delicious with small bread croûtons scattered on top.

Mix the marinade ingredients together. Place the meat in a shallow
bowl, and pour the marinade on top. Turn the meat, and be sure to
dab the marinade all over it. Sprinkle chopped cress over the entire
surface. Cover with plastic wrap and refrigerate for 48 hours.

Scrape off the spices and cress. Place the meat in a plastic bag and
refrigerate for another 48 hours.

For the sauce, mix all the ingredients together, stirring thoroughly
and adding the oil slowly. If required, dilute the sauce with a couple of
spoonfuls of water or a little lemon juice.

Slice the beef thinly with a very sharp knife. Serve together with the
spicy sauce.

Springtime celebrations for young girls in Sweden.

POTATO DUMPLINGS
STUFFED WITH BACON
KROPPKAKOR

SERVES 4–6

12–14 medium potatoes, about
   2lb
2–3 eggs
1–1¼ cups flour
1–1½ tsp salt
9 cups salted water
melted butter, to serve

STUFFING

5–7oz unsmoked bacon, cubed
5–7oz smoked bacon, cubed
2 onions, chopped
½ tsp black pepper

Potato dumplings with a difference! The salty, smoky taste of the bacon and onion filling is a delicious surprise inside the smooth-textured dumpling.

Boil the potatoes until tender, then cool and mash. To make the stuffing, brown the bacon and onions in a pan. Season with pepper and cool. Mix the mashed potatoes with the eggs, flour, and salt. Knead into a dough, then shape into a thick roll. Cut into 12–14 slices.

Make a large hollow in each dumpling, fill with the bacon stuffing and enclose it. Shape into balls and press flat. Bring the salted water to the boil. Lower the dumplings, a few at a time, into the salted water. Boil for 5 minutes, or until they float to the surface. Serve with melted butter.

Potato dumplings stuffed with bacon ▶

PTARMIGAN (GROUSE)
RYPER

SERVES 3

3 ptarmigans
3 thin slices of lard or fat bacon
2 tbsp butter
salt and pepper

SAUCE

2 tbsp flour
1¼ cups stock
1 ptarmigan liver, chopped
½ cup cream or sour cream
¼ cup redcurrant jelly

Game is a favorite with Norwegians. This method of preparation keeps the meat moist and succulent. The sharpness of the redcurrant jelly adds just the right piquancy to the sauce.

Clean and dry the ptarmigans. Place a slice of lard or fat bacon underneath the skin of the breast. Truss the ptarmigans as for chicken. Brown the ptarmigans on all sides in the butter in a pan. Season with salt and pepper. Pour about 1 cup boiling water into the pan, then let ptarmigans simmer over a low heat for 45–60 minutes until tender. Remove the ptarmigans, and keep warm.

For the sauce, stir the flour into some cold water. Add to the stock and simmer for 5 minutes. Add the liver to the sauce. Pour in the cream, and add the redcurrant jelly to taste.

MEAT LOAF EN CROUTE
INBAKAD KÖTTFÄRS

SERVES 4–6

PASTRY

2½ cups flour

1 cup butter or margarine

3 tbsp cold water

MEAT CASE

⅓ cup dried breadcrumbs

½ cup cream

½ cup water

½ onion, chopped

butter for frying

14oz ground beef, veal or pork,
  as available

1½ tsp white pepper

FILLING

¼lb frozen chicken livers, thawed

½ tsp salt

½ tsp pepper

The chicken liver filling adds a gourmet touch to the meat loaf.
An attractive dish which tastes as good as it looks.

For the pastry, mix the butter or margarine into the flour and combine with water to make a dough. Leave in the refrigerator for 1 hour.

Mix the breadcrumbs with the cream and water. Fry the onion in a little butter. Slice the chicken livers, fry and season. Mix the minced meat with salt, pepper, breadcrumb mixture and fried onion. Pat the mixture into a meat loaf shape on moistened greaseproof paper. Cut a line along the top and fill with the livers, then smooth over to cover.

Preheat the oven to 220°C/425°F/Gas Mark 7. Roll out the pastry between sheets of cling film. Remove the cling film now and then to sprinkle with flour. Roll out one rectangle large enough to wrap around the meat loaf. Trim away uneven edges and save for decoration.

Ease the meat loaf on to the pastry. First fold up the short ends, trimming away the pastry at the corners so that it is not too thick. Fold up the long sides but not too tightly. Seal the join. Ease the parcel onto a greased baking sheet. Decorate with pastry trimmings. Bake for 30–35 minutes.

If liked, served with chopped iceberg lettuce and peppers dressed in a mixture of 3 tbsp mayonnaise, 2 tbsp tomato purée, 45ml/3 tbsp water, salt and pepper.

Meat loaf en croute ▶

BRAISED VENISON
PORONKARISTYS

SERVES 4–6

¾lb bacon

butter for cooking

3lb venison

1 tbsp salt

10 whole allspice

1¼ cups water

In Finland this would be made with reindeer meat, but venison
is just as good. The most common seasonings are green and
black pepper, allspice, bay leaves, and salt.

Cut the bacon into thin strips. Melt the butter in a saucepan, and brown the bacon. Cut the venison into thin strips, add a little at a time to the bacon, and brown. Add the seasoning and water. Cover and cook slowly for about 30 minutes, until tender. Serve with mashed potatoes, cranberries, and beer, homemade if possible.

MEAT CAKES

KJOTTKAKER

Ginger and nutmeg gives these meat cakes their distinctive flavor.

SERVES 4

1lb 2oz ground beef

¾ tbsp salt

¼lb suet, finely chopped

2 tbsp potato flour or cornstarch

1¾–2¼ cups cold water or milk

pinch of pepper, ginger, and
grated nutmeg

2 tbsp wholewheat flour

¼ cup butter for frying

2¼ cups boiling water

1 onion

Mix the meat with the salt, suet, and potato flour. Stir well in one direction only. Gradually add the cold water or milk until the mix becomes firm in texture. Add all the spices.

Dab each meat cake in flour and fry until brown. Place in a saucepan as they are ready. Add the boiling water and simmer for about 15 minutes. Blanch the onion and cut into slices. Brown, then simmer in the cooking liquid. A sauce may be made by browning butter and flour, gradually adding the cooking water or stock.

Meat cakes ▶

DUMPLINGS
MELBOLLER

Dumplings are a very big part of traditional Danish cooking, especially in the countryside. They are often served with meat as well as in hot or cold soups.

SERVES 4–6

⅓ cup butter

½ cup flour

½ cup boiling water

2 eggs, separated

½ tsp salt

¼ tsp sugar

Melt the butter and stir in the flour, adding the boiling water gradually. Cool the mixture.

Whisk the egg whites until stiff. Add the yolks, salt, and sugar to the cold mixture. Fold in the egg whites. Form into small balls. Cook the dumplings slowly in boiling water for a few minutes. Serve with most soups.

ROBERTO'S VEAL ROULADES
ROBERTOS KALVRULADER

SERVES 4

1lb 6oz thick flank of veal, thinly sliced

2oz mushrooms, finely chopped

¼lb ground pork

1 tbsp grated parmesan cheese

1 slice of white bread, grated

1 egg, beaten

1 tbsp chopped fresh parsley

1 tsp sage

salt and pepper

butter for cooking

1–2 medium onions, sliced

1 carrot, sliced

1¼ cups white wine

2 tbsp tomato paste

arrowroot for thickening

This is a traditional Swedish dish. It is as popular in restaurants as it is for dinner parties at home.

Beat the veal slices as thinly as possible and cut in half. Mix together the mushrooms, ground pork, cheese, grated bread, egg, parsley, sage, salt, and pepper.

Spread the filling over the veal slices, then carefully roll them up. Hold the roulades together with toothpicks. Brown all over in butter in a frying pan, then transfer them to a flameproof casserole dish. Add the onions and carrot.

Boil the wine and tomato paste in the frying pan, and pour into the casserole. Simmer, covered, for 30–40 minutes. Dilute, if required, with a little warm water. Strain the juices, thicken with a little arrowroot, adjust the seasoning, and pour back over the roulades. Serve with boiled rice or potatoes and a green salad.

Roberto's veal roulades ▶

KARELIAN STEW
KARJALANPAISTI

SERVES 4–6

1lb pork

1lb mutton

1lb beef

1½ tbsp salt

15–20 whole allspice

2 onions, sliced

5 cups beef stock

Karelia is eastern Finland, and this Karelian stew is an easy start to get acquainted with the eastern flavors. As with all slowly cooked stews, this dish is best cooked a day ahead. Refrigerate and skim off the fat. Reheat in the oven at a medium heat for about 30 minutes, until piping hot.

Preheat the oven to 300°F. Cut the meat into 1-inch cubes and place in a casserole dish. Add the salt, allspice, and onions to the casserole. Add sufficient beef stock to cover the meat. Cook until tender, 30–40 minutes, stirring occasionally. Cover the dish with a lid toward the end of the cooking time. Serve with mashed potatoes.

MEATBALLS
KÖTTBULLAR

SERVES 4–6

7 tbsp breadcrumbs

1 ¼ cups cream and water mixture

¾ lb ground beef

¼ lb ground veal

¼ lb ground pork

1 onion, chopped

3 tbsp butter

salt and pepper

No smörgåsbord is complete without meatballs. This dish is very versatile; it goes with everything and is seen everywhere. There are as many recipes as there are cooks.

Soak the breadcrumbs in the cream and water mixture. Mix together the ground beef, veal, and pork. Fry the onion in a little of the butter until golden brown. Mix together the meat, onion, egg, and soaked breadcrumbs. Work the meat thoroughly until it is smooth, then season with salt and pepper.

Shape into balls, and fry a few at a time in the remaining butter. Meatballs can be served with meat or chicken, in a soup, or on their own, hot or cold.

SWEETBREADS WITH GARLIC MAYONNAISE
KALVEBRISSEL MED HVITLØKMAJONES

SERVES 4

10oz sweetbreads

boiled rice or lettuce leaves,
   to serve

STOCK

2 ¼ cups water

½ tsp salt

5 peppercorns

sprig of parsley

1 carrot, sliced

½ onion, sliced

1 bay leaf

GARLIC MAYONNAISE

⅔ cup mayonnaise

¼ cup sour cream

1 clove garlic, crushed

2 tbsp chopped fresh parsley,
   dill, and chives

The delicate taste of sweetbreads is enhanced by the garlic mayonnaise.

Place the sweetbreads in cold water and bring to the boil. Drain, then remove any dark parts and outer membranes. Bring all the stock ingredients to the boil, and simmer for about 10 minutes. Place the sweetbreads in the stock, and simmer for a further 10 minutes. Leave to cool in the stock.

Mix the mayonnaise and sour cream, garlic, parsley, dill, and chives together. Cut the sweetbreads in slices. Place them on a bed of boiled rice or lettuce leaves. Pour a little mayonnaise on each slice. Serve with toasted bread and butter.

GOURMET LAMB

VORSCHMACK

SERVES 4–6

1 soaked salt herring, or 2 Matjes
herring fillets

8 anchovy fillets

2lb roast lamb

2 medium onions

½ tbsp butter for cooking

juice from the roast lamb or
consommé

1 tbsp tomato sauce or paste

white pepper

2 tbsp mustard

½ cup light cream

*Originating from Poland, Vorschmack was a favorite of
Finland's national hero Field Marshall Mannerheim. It is very
tasty as an appertizer or a late evening snack.*

Clean and fillet the herring. Grind the fillets, anchovies, roast lamb,
and onions in a grinder or food processor.

Melt the butter in a saucepan, add the meat mixture, and bring to
the boil. Add a little meat juice or consommé until the mixture
becomes porridge-like in consistency. Add the tomato sauce or paste
and pepper to taste. Add the mustard and cream.

Simmer the lamb for 30 minutes, stirring occasionally to prevent
sticking. Serve steaming hot with pickled cucumbers, pickled beet, and
sour cream. The traditional drink Ryyppy (see below) is served ice cold
as an accompaniment to the meal.

RYYPPY

2 cups aquavit

2 cups vodka

scant 1 cup Noilly Prat vermouth

scant ½ cup gin

*This is a very traditional Finnish drink – and an extremely
intoxicating one! It is served with Gourmet Lamb among other
dishes.*

Mix all the ingredients in a shaker and fill the glasses to the brim.

*Fishermen returning to Oddenhaven in
Denmark with their catch.*

VENISON WITH GOAT'S CHEESE
DYRESTEG

SERVES 4–6

3lb venison joint

3 tbsp softened butter

salt and ground black pepper

2½ cups beef stock

1 tbsp butter

1 tbsp flour

2 tsp redcurrant jelly

6oz goat's cheese, diced

⅓ cup sour cream

Reindeer meat is hard to find outside Scandinavia, but venison is more readily available so this traditional recipe has been prepared here with venison. Prepared this way the meat will remain succulent. The sauce adds a special gourmet touch to this Norwegian specialty.

Preheat the oven to 475°F. Tie the joint with string to keep its shape during cooking. Brush the meat with the softened butter. Place the meat on a rack in a roasting pan. Roast for 20 minutes. Lower the oven heat to 350°F. Season generously with salt and a pinch of black pepper. Pour in the stock and roast for another hour, basting with the stock a few times.

Remove the meat and place in an ovenproof dish. Leave in the turned off oven with the door open. Skim the fat off the meat juice in the pan. Measure out 1 cup meat juice, topping up with water if needed. Reheat.

Melt the 1 tbsp butter and stir in the flour. Cook for 2–3 minutes on a low heat, stirring continuously. Whisk in the meat juice, then add the redcurrant jelly and diced goat's cheese. Keep whisking until the sauce is smooth. Add the sour cream and warm through, but do not let the sauce come to the boil. Season to taste. Slice the meat thinly, and serve with the sauce.

Children during their Easter festivities in Finland.

SUMMER OMELET WITH SAUSAGES

SOMMERAEGGEHAGE MED POLSER

SERVES 4–6

6 tomatoes

½ cucumber

12 radishes

chives

5 frankfurters

5 tbsp butter

8 eggs

½ cup milk or light cream

pepper

It is the way in which this omelet is served that makes it typically Danish. Another example of a tasty dish, made with the easily obtainable canned Danish frankfurters.

Slice the tomatoes, cucumber, and radishes, and chop the chives.

Slice the frankfurters and sauté in 1 tbsp of the butter. Beat the eggs a little, and whisk in the milk or cream. Season with pepper. Heat the remaining butter in a nonstick frying pan, and pour in the egg mixture. Add the sliced frankfurters, cook, and stir constantly until set. Season to taste.

Serve the omelet on a serving dish surrounded by the tomatoes, cucumber, and radishes. Sprinkle the chives on top.

PALACE STEAK

SLOTTSSTEK

SERVES 4–6

1¾lb boneless beef (fillet
  or thick flank)

1 tbsp butter

1 tsp salt

6 whole allspice

6 white peppercorns

1 tsp pickling vinegar

1½ tbsp corn syrup

3–4 anchovy fillets

1 medium onion, chopped

1 bay leaf

1¼ cups stock

¼ cups port

The traditional Swedish Palace Steak acquires its characteristic flavor from bay leaves, anchovies, and a little pickling vinegar, similar to the Swedish beef stew.

Brown the steak on both sides in melted butter in a flameproof casserole. Sprinkle the salt on the meat, and place the remaining spices, vinegar, syrup, anchovy fillets, onion, and bay leaf in the casserole. Add some of the stock, together with the port. Reduce the heat to low and cover. Simmer for 1½ hours. Add more stock during cooking, and turn the meat occasionally. Test that the meat is cooked through.

Sieve the gravy into a saucepan. Whisk the flour into a little water and add to thicken the gravy. Boil for a few minutes with the bay leaf, and add the cream. Season to taste.

Slice the meat and cut into portions. Serve with boiled or sauté potatoes, fresh vegetables, the sauce, and loganberry or black or redcurrant jelly.

SAUCE

1¾ cups beef gravy	1 bay leaf
1½ tbsp flour	few peppercorns
¼–½ cup light cream	salt and pepper

◄ *Palace steak*

LAMB AND CABBAGE STEW

FÅR I KÅL

SERVES 4

2lb lamb on the bone, such as
  middle neck or breast

2lb white cabbage

2–3 tbsp butter

1–2 tsp salt

10 white peppercorns

1 bay leaf

2 cups water

chopped fresh parsley

Wholesome and warming, this stew uses economical cuts of lamb, is easy to prepare, and has a real country flavor.

Trim the meat and cut into large cubes. Cut the cabbage into large pieces. Brown the meat and cabbage in the butter.

Alternate layers of meat and cabbage in a flameproof casserole dish. Sprinkle each layer with salt and pepper. Add the bay leaf and water. Cover the pan, and bring to the boil. Skim off the fat, then simmer for 1½ hours or until tender. Sprinkle with chopped parsley, and serve with boiled potatoes.

SWEDISH HASH

PYTT I PANNA

A useful way to deal with leftover meat. The smoked sausage or ham adds a distinctive flavor.

SERVES 4–6

2–3 tbsp butter

2 medium onions, finely chopped

¾lb smoked sausage or ham, diced

8 boiled potatoes, diced

3 cups leftover meat, diced

salt and pepper

chopped fresh parsley

Melt half of the butter in a frying pan, and gently fry the onions until golden brown. Remove to a platter, and add the remaining butter to the pan. Fry the smoked sausage or ham together with the diced potatoes. Add the fried onions and diced leftover meat. Mix gently. Season to taste, and heat thoroughly. Sprinkle the chopped parsley on top. Serve piping hot with raw egg yolk or fried egg, fresh cucumber salad, or pickled beets.

Swedish hash ▶

MEAT PATTIES
FRIKADELLER

Frikadeller are as Danish as their flag, Danneborg, and there are endless variations. This dish can be eaten either hot or cold.

SERVES 4–6

¼ cup butter

2 tbsp oil

1 medium onion, chopped

½ lb ground veal

½ lb ground pork

3 tbsp flour

1½ cups soda water

1 egg

1 tsp salt

pepper

Melt a little of the butter and oil, and fry the onion until golden brown. Mix the ground veal and pork together in a bowl with the flour. Slowly stir in the soda water until the mixture is light and fluffy. Add the onion to the bowl. Whisk in the egg, salt, and pepper, cover the bowl, and leave to cool for 1 hour.

Form the meat mixture into balls or hamburger shapes. Melt the remaining butter and oil, and fry the patties for about 15 minutes. Serve with boiled potatoes, pickled beets or red cabbage.

EASTER CHICKEN CASSEROLE
PASKEKYLLING MED AEGGARNITURE

SERVES 4–6

¼ cup butter

3lb chicken joints

3 medium onions, chopped

2½ cups chicken stock

½lb mushrooms

2 tbsp chopped fresh parsley

salt and pepper

2 cups peas

2 eggs

2 tbsp milk

butter for cooking

2 tbsp cornstarch

This dish is traditionally served on Easter Monday with decorated eggs, new potatoes, carrots, and peas, followed by a cheese board and a dessert.

Melt the butter and fry the chicken joints and onions until golden brown. Add the chicken stock, mushrooms, and 1 tbsp of the chopped parsley, and season with salt and pepper. Cover and simmer for 35 minutes, adding the peas for the last 5–8 minutes.

Beat the eggs and milk together and season. Fry the egg mixture in a little butter in an omelet pan until firm. Put the chicken and vegetables on a heated serving dish and keep warm. Thicken the cooking liquid with the cornstarch blended with water to make the gravy. Pour the gravy over the chicken and vegetables. Cut the fried egg into thin strips, and use to garnish the chicken, along with the remaining chopped parsley.

Easter chicken casserole ▶

LIVER AND RICE CASSEROLE
MAKSALAATIKKO

SERVES 6–8

1¾ cups white long grain rice

1 gallon boiling salted water

3 tbsp butter

1 medium onion, finely chopped

2 cups milk

2 eggs, lightly beaten

4 bacon slices, cooked and diced

⅔ cup raisins

2 tbsp corn syrup

2 tsp salt

1 tsp white pepper

1 tsp ground marjoram

1½lb calf's or ox liver, finely
  chopped

The baking oven came from the east more than a thousand years ago, and the old, tried and true Finnish dishes still depend on it. In fact, most Finnish cooking makes heavy use of the oven.

Cook the rice in the boiling salted water for about 12 minutes, then drain and put aside. Melt 2 tbsp butter in a frying pan, and gently sauté the onion until golden. Remove and put aside.

Preheat the oven to 325°F. In a large bowl, carefully combine the cooked rice, the milk, and beaten eggs. Add the onion, diced bacon, raisins, and corn syrup. Season with salt, pepper, and marjoram. Stir in the chopped liver and mix thoroughly.

Grease an ovenproof dish, and add the liver and rice mixture. Bake, uncovered, for 1–1½ hours. Serve with green salad and either loganberry or cranberry sauce.

ROAST GOOSE

GAASE STEG

SERVES 8–10

1½ cups prunes, pitted

9–10lb goose

juice of 1 lemon

2 medium apples, cored and
  peeled

1 tbsp salt

2½ cups chicken stock or water

1 tbsp sugar

pepper

The main dish at the Christmas table is roast goose. Danish tradition demands the goose be stuffed with peeled and sliced apples and prunes. It is served with cooked apples stuffed with prunes, and the recipe for this is on page 86.

Soak the prunes in water for 12 hours. Preheat the oven to 350°F. Rinse the goose thoroughly under cold running water. Dry with paper towels. Brush the goose both inside and out with the juice from the lemon, and then rub the inside of the goose with the sugar, pepper, and onion. Cut the prunes and apples into small pieces, sprinkle with salt, and place inside the goose. Secure with skewers, or sew the skin together. Sprinkle with salt. Place the goose in a baking pan and put it on the bottom oven shelf. Roast for about 20 minutes to brown.

Drain off the fat and pour the boiling stock or water, sugar, and pepper into the pan. Turn the goose over so the back is facing up, and roast for 1 hour. Turn it breast up and roast for a farther 1½–2 hours. Leave for 15 minutes in the switched off oven with the door open. Remove the stuffing and discard it – it is too fatty to eat.

Serve the goose with apples stuffed with prunes (page 86), red cabbage (page 82), and caramelized potatoes (page 94).

*A traditional, thatched-roof barn in
Skansen, Stockholm.*

GROUSE WITH CREAM SAUCE

RIEKKO KERMAKASTIKKEESSA

SERVES 4–6

1–2 tbsp butter

2 grouse, cleaned

2 tsp salt

¼ tsp pepper

scant 2 cups consommé

SAUCE

about 1 cup juice from
   the birds

2–3 tbsp flour

1 cup cream

salt

Finns love the taste of game – some even prepare chicken to taste like game by rubbing it inside and out with a mixture of chopped pine needles and juniper berries. The chicken is then left to hang for a few days before roasting it to get the flavor of game.

Melt the butter in a frying pan and fry the birds. Sprinkle with salt and pepper. Add the consommé, and bring to the boil. Reduce the heat, then simmer for about 45 minutes until tender. Keep the birds warm.

Strain the juice from the frying pan into a saucepan, whisk in the flour, and heat gently. Add the juice from the birds, whisking all the time. Stir in the cream, and season to taste. Simmer for a few minutes.

Remove the meat from the bones, and place in a heated serving dish. Pour the cream sauce over the birds. Serve with boiled potatoes, vegetables, mushrooms, and either berries or redcurrant jelly.

EASTER VEAL

PASKEKALV

SERVES 4–6

2lb boneless leg of veal

5 cups veal or chicken stock

5 carrots, sliced

15 shallots or very small onions

bouquet garni of 5 sprigs of
   parsley, 1 stick of sliced celery,
   1 bay leaf, 4 white
   peppercorns, and ¼ tsp thyme,
   tied in cheesecloth

1½ tsp salt

¼ cup butter

¼ cup flour

2 egg yolks, beaten

1½ tbsp lemon juice

½lb mushrooms, sautéed

This is another traditional dish, very often served during Easter celebrations.

Boil the meat for 5 minutes in water, ensuring the meat is covered. Remove the froth and drain. Put the meat into a deep saucepan and add the stock, carrots, shallots, and the bouquet garni. Add a little salt. Bring to the boil, skimming off any froth. Simmer for 1–11/2 hours until tender.

Remove the meat, carrots, and shallots. Strain the liquid. Melt the butter, add the flour, and cook for 2–3 minutes, stirring continuously. Gradually add the stock, stirring until the mixture is thick and smooth. Remove from the heat. Add the beaten egg yolks with the lemon juice. Stir in the sautéed mushrooms. Slice the meat, and serve with rice or mashed potatoes.

CREAMED SWEETBREADS

KALVBRÄSS

SERVES 4–6

1 lb sweetbreads

2–4 tbsp butter

1 medium carrot, sliced

1 small onion

1 bay leaf

¼ tsp dried thyme

sprig of parsley

4–5 white peppercorns

2¼ cup chicken stock or water

butter for cooking

1–2 tbsp flour

1¼ cups heavy or whipping cream

salt and pepper

sherry (optional)

Delicious served on its own or on toast, but superlative as a filling for omelets or tiny puff pastry cases. The preparation is simple, and the result is delicious – well worth the time spent.

Clean the sweetbreads, removing any blood vessels and membranes. Soak in cold water for about 1 hour. Bring to the boil in lightly salted water. Rinse under cold running water.

Put a knob of butter, the carrot, onion, bay leaf, thyme, parsley, and peppercorns into a saucepan. Place the sweetbreads on top, and leave to sweat over a low heat for 5 minutes. Cover the sweetbreads with chicken stock or water, and add salt to taste. Place a lid on the saucepan, and boil for 10 minutes.

Put the sweetbreads in a bowl, and strain the liquid over them. Leave to cool. Cut the sweetbreads into small pieces, and fry lightly in the remaining butter. Sprinkle with the flour, and continue to fry lightly for a few minutes. Add the cream, stirring continuously until thick and smooth. Season with salt and pepper; you may add a little sherry, if you wish, for taste.

Café society in the streets of Copenhagen.

FILLET OF VEAL A LA OSCAR

KALVFILE OSCAR

SERVES 4–6

6 slices of veal fillet or thick flank
(1¼–1½lb)

salt and white pepper

2 tbsp flour for coating

2 tbsp butter

1 small can asparagus tips

1 small cooked lobster, or 1 can
crab meat

CHORON SAUCE

2 tbsp vinegar

1 tbsp water

6 crushed white peppercorns

1 tbsp finely chopped onion

a few parsley stalks

½ tsp dried tarragon

½ tsp dried chervil

3 egg yolks

scant 1 cup butter or margarine

2 tbsp tomato paste

This dish, with its royal connotations, as the name suggests, should be made from fillet of veal with lobster and asparagus to garnish. But as veal fillet is expensive, thick flank can be used instead, with apologies to King Oscar.

For the sauce, mix the vinegar, water, peppercorns, onion, and herbs in a heavy saucepan. Bring to the boil, and reduce by half. Strain, and pour back into the pan. Stand the pan in a baking dish half filled with simmering water and add the yolks, whisking hard. Continue whisking until the mixture is thick and fluffy. Melt the butter or margarine, then pour into the mixture slowly, whisking vigorously. Add the tomato paste, a little at a time. Leave the sauce to keep warm in the baking dish while the meat is being prepared.

Flatten the meat slices, season with salt and pepper, then coat in the flour. Fry in a pan in half the butter for 4 minutes on each side. Place on a warm serving dish.

Warm the asparagus in the remaining butter. Place a couple of asparagus tips, with a few pieces of lobster meat or crab meat and one or two tablespoons of Choron Sauce, with each slice of meat. Serve with sauté potatoes and salad.

PIGS' FEET

SIANSORKKA

SERVES 4–6

4–5lb pigs' feet, preferably
forelegs

1 gallon water

4 tsp salt

20 whole white peppercorns

2–3 bay leaves

Lent is traditionally a time for outdoor get-togethers, where lanterns and candles are placed in trees. It requires food that can be prepared beforehand.

Rinse the pigs' feet well in cold water. Place in a saucepan, cover with the cold water and bring to the boil. Skim off any foam, and season with the salt, peppercorns, and bay leaves. Simmer over low heat for 2–3 hours, until tender. Leave to cool in the pan. Remove and serve cold. This dish is easiest eaten with your fingers.

5

VEGETABLE DISHES AND SALADS

Fresh mushroom salad

Jansson's temptation

Red cabbage

Hot potato salad with bacon

Chicory au gratin

Swede casserole

Lacy potato pancakes with chives

Cooked apples stuffed with prunes

Potato cake with rosemary

Button mushroom and broccoli gratin

Stuffed onions

Vegetable salad

Coleslaw

West Coast salad

Kale in cream sauce

Caramelized potatoes

FRESH MUSHROOM SALAD
SIENISALAATTI

SERVES 4–6

¾ cup water

1 tbsp lemon juice

½lb fresh mushrooms, sliced

¼ cup heavy cream

1 tbsp grated onion

pinch of sugar

2 tsp salt

½ tsp white pepper

lettuce leaves

As with wild berries, picking mushrooms is universally enjoyed. Each mushroom has its own shape, taste, and character. There are hundreds of edible varieties. Mushrooms can be used in salads, soups, and sauces.

Bring the water and lemon juice to the boil. Add the mushrooms, and cover. Reduce the heat, and simmer for 2–3 minutes. Drain the mushrooms, and dry on paper towels.

In a bowl, mix the cream, onion, sugar, salt, and pepper, then toss the mushrooms in the mixture. Serve on crisp, dry lettuce leaves.

Fresh mushroom salad ▶

JANSSON'S TEMPTATION
JANSSONS FRESTELSE

SERVES 4–6

6 medium potatoes

10 anchovies in brine

2 medium onions, thinly sliced

2–4 tbsp butter

generous 1 cup heavy cream

No wonder Jansson was tempted! The saltiness of the anchovies is tempered by the potatoes. Onions add a contrasting flavor and the cream makes this dish irresistible.

Preheat the oven to 325°F. Peel the potatoes and cut into thin strips. Soak them in cold water to get rid of the starch – it will make the potatoes crispier. Meanwhile, cut the anchovy fillets in half, if preferred. Reserve the brine. Fry the onions gently in half the butter until golden brown.

Grease an ovenproof dish. Dry the potatoes with paper towels. Put the potatoes, anchovies, and onions in layers, beginning and finishing with potato. Pour over half of the cream. Dot with the remaining butter and pour over 4 tbsp anchovy brine. Bake for about 25 minutes. Pour over the rest of the cream and anchovy brine, then bake for another 20 minutes. Serve with cold beer.

RED CABBAGE

RØDKAAL

SERVES 4–6

3lb red cabbage

3 tbsp butter

1–2 tbsp sugar

¼ cup water

¼ cup malt vinegar

salt and pepper

2 medium tart apples

⅔ cup redcurrant jelly

This piquant, colorful dish complements most menus very well. Red cabbage tastes better if made the day before, then reheated. Equally delicious served cold, it's popular in Denmark on the day after Christmas.

Shred the cabbage. Melt the butter in a large frying pan, and stir in the sugar. Add the cabbage and cook for 5 minutes, stirring continuously. Add the water, vinegar, salt, and pepper. Cover and simmer for 2–3 hours, until tender. Peel and grate the apples, and add to the cabbage along with the redcurrant jelly.

The lake at Oldevatre – Norway's beautiful wilderness at its best.

HOT POTATO SALAD WITH BACON

VARM POTETSALAT MED BACON

SERVES 4

5 bacon slices

8–10 cold boiled potatoes, sliced

1 medium onion, finely chopped

2 tbsp chopped fresh parsley

1–1½ tbsp wine vinegar

1–2 tbsp water

salt and pepper

Hot potato salad, flavored with bacon pieces and sharpened with hint of wine vinegar, is a tasty way to serve potatoes. It is quick and easy to prepare, and very good to serve with sausages or other meats.

Cut the bacon slices into small strips, and fry until crisp. Place the potatoes and other ingredients in the frying pan. Stir carefully to mix. Place the lid on the pan, and heat the salad carefully for 5–6 minutes. The potatoes must not brown. Serve with meat and sausages.

CHICORY AU GRATIN
GRATINERAD ENDIVE

SERVES 2

about 4 chicory spears, sliced

¼lb ham, cubed (about 1 cup)

¼ cup butter

2 tbsp flour

1¼ cups hot milk

salt and pepper

1 tbsp tomato paste or red wine

grated cheese for topping

A very tasty gratin using ham, or bacon if preferred. Alternatively, use smoked fish or shrimp to give it a totally different, but nonetheless delicious character. If shrimp are used, substitute ½ cup white wine for ½ cup of the milk.

Place a layer of sliced chicory in an ovenproof dish. Sprinkle with fried cubes of ham.

Melt half the butter, add the flour, and cook for 2–3 minutes, stirring. Gradually stir in the hot milk. Season the sauce with salt and pepper, and a little tomato paste or red wine. Pour over the chicory. Sprinkle plenty of grated cheese on top, and dot with the remaining butter. Bake for about 20 minutes, until the chicory is cooked and the topping is golden.

SWEDE CASSEROLE
LANTTULAATIKKO

SERVES 4–6

2 medium swedes or 2lb turnips, peeled

1½ tsp salt

4 tsp breadcrumbs

¼ cup heavy cream

½ tsp grated nutmeg

2 eggs, lightly beaten

2 tbsp butter

This casserole is delicious, but, in fact, any vegetables can be used. If made with carrots only, it is called Porkhanalaatikko.

Dice the swedes into ¼-inch pieces, and put into a saucepan. Cover with cold water, add ½ tsp of the salt, and bring to the boil. Lower the heat, and simmer for about 20 minutes until soft. Drain the swedes, and purée in a blender.

Preheat the oven to 325°F. Soak the breadcrumbs in the cream for a few minutes. Stir in the nutmeg, remaining salt, and the beaten eggs. Add the puréed swede, and mix thoroughly.

Grease a large casserole dish, and pour in the mixture. Cut the butter into tiny pieces, and dot over the swedes. Bake, uncovered, for about 1 hour, until golden brown. Serve with meat or fish, or on its own.

LACY POTATO PANCAKES WITH CHIVES

RÅRAKOR

SERVES 4–6

4 medium potatoes

2 tbsp chopped fresh chives

2 tbsp salt

freshly ground black pepper

2 tbsp butter

2 tbsp vegetable oil

Chives add the flavor of spring to this dish, and the crispy, lacy texture provided by the grated potatoes makes these pancakes delightfully different.

Peel the potatoes, and grate them coarsely into a large bowl. Do not drain off the potato water that accumulates in the bowl. Working quickly to prevent the potatoes from turning brown, add the chopped chives, salt, and a little pepper.

Heat the butter and oil in a 10-inch frying pan. When very hot, add 2 tbsp potato mixture for each pancake. Fry on both sides for 2–3 minutes, until golden brown. Flatten them with a spatula during cooking. Serve straight away.

COOKED APPLES STUFFED WITH PRUNES

KOGT AEBLER MED SVEDSKER

SERVES 4–8

1 cup sugar

port to taste

16 prunes

8 large apples, cored and peeled

4 cups cold water

Serve these port-flavored prune and apple halves hot with goose or duck.

Put 2 tsp sugar, the port, and prunes in an ovenproof dish. Leave to macerate for 6–8 hours. Preheat the oven to 325°F. Cook for 20–30 minutes, until soft.

Cut the apples in half. Mix the remaining sugar and water in a pan then boil for 2–3 minutes. Add the apples, and leave to simmer for 10 minutes, uncovered, over a low heat. Remove the apples with a slotted spoon, and place in a serving dish. Put one prune on each apple half

POTATO CAKE WITH ROSEMARY

POTETKAKE MED ROSMARIN

SERVES 4–6

8 potatoes

¼ cup margarine or butter

1 tsp fresh or ½ tsp dried rosemary

1½ tsp salt

A simple but delicious way to serve potatoes. Pressing the potatoes together while cooking forms a crisp "cake."

Peel the potatoes and slice thinly. Rinse and dry them well. Melt the margarine or butter in a frying pan, and brown the potato slices carefully. Sprinkle with the rosemary and salt.

Carefully press the potato slices together, and fry them over a low heat until they are tender and the cake has a nice color underneath. Turn the cake over, and fry until lightly browned. This can be served with either meat or fish dishes.

BUTTON MUSHROOM
AND BROCCOLI GRATIN
KANTARELLGRATINERT BROCCOLI

SERVES 4–6

1 lb fresh broccoli

salt

SAUCE

½ lb button mushrooms

1 tbsp butter

1½ tbsp flour

1¼ cups cream

½–1 tsp salt

1 tbsp grated cheese

A gratin of broccoli with button mushrooms – a simple dish retaining the full flavor of the vegetables.

Boil the broccoli in salted water until tender. Drain, and place in a buttered, ovenproof dish. Cut the mushrooms into small pieces, and fry them quickly in the butter. Drain any liquid into a separate container. Sprinkle the mushrooms with the flour, stirring. Add the cream and reserved liquid, and boil for a couple of minutes, stirring. Pour over the broccoli, and sprinkle with the cheese. Brown for 5–8 minutes. Serve with meat or fish, or on its own.

STUFFED ONIONS
LÖKDOLMAR

SERVES 4–6

3–4 large yellow onions

1 tbsp breadcrumbs

½ cup light cream

5 oz ground veal,
  or 1 cup cooked rice

1 small can of mushrooms

1 egg yolk

salt and white pepper

celery salt

2 tbsp butter

These old-fashioned stuffed onions are a delicacy, well worth a revival in their popularity. It is difficult to understand why this fine dish has been forgotten.

Peel the onions, and make a deep cut through half of each onion. Boil the onions until semi-soft in lightly salted water. Drain, reserving the cooking liquid, then rinse them under cold water. Separate the layers carefully and leave to drain. Take the cores of the onions and chop finely.

Stir the breadcrumbs into the cream, and leave to swell. Mix with the veal or rice, mushrooms, chopped onion cores, and egg yolk. Season well with salt, pepper, and celery salt.

Place 1 tbsp of the mixture on every large onion layer and fold. Melt the butter in a frying pan, and brown the stuffed onion layers all over. Add ⅔ cup of the onion water and simmer, covered, until soft. Add more onion water, if needed.

Stuffed onions can also be baked in a greased ovenproof dish. First brush with melted butter or margarine, then bake in the oven at 425°F for 30 minutes.

Stuffed onions ▶

VEGETABLE SALAD

ROSOLLI

Rosolli is very often eaten as a great savory pick-me-up on Christmas Eve morning.

SERVES 6

7 fresh beets

5 potatoes

7 carrots

2 apples

2 medium onions

3 large sprigs fresh dill, or
   1½ tsp dill seed

salt

Boil the beets and potatoes in their skins with the carrots until tender. Refrigerate for 2–3 hours. Peel and chop the cooked vegetables, apples, and onions, and chop the dill. Mix them all together, and season with salt, tossing a few times. Serve with mayonnaise.

Vegetable salad ▶

COLESLAW
VITKÅLS SALAD

So easy to prepare, the taste of this coleslaw is much more individual than supermarket versions. It is a healthy accompaniment to cold meats.

SERVES 4–6

1 small cabbage

1 small leek

5–6 carrots

6 pickled gherkins

DRESSING

½ cup oil

½ cup cider vinegar

¼ cup sugar (or less sugar with a spoonful of honey)

1 tsp salt

1½ tsp coarsely ground black pepper

a little lemon juice

Finely shred the cabbage and leek. Coarsely grate the carrots, and chop the gherkins.

Bring the dressing ingredients to the boil in a saucepan. Pour the hot dressing over the vegetables. Serve cold.

WEST COAST SALAD
VÄSTKUSTSALLAD

SERVES 4–6

½lb cooked fresh shrimp

1 cooked fresh lobster or crab, or
   6oz canned

2 tomatoes

¼lb mushrooms, sliced

1 lettuce, shredded

1 small can asparagus and/or
   1 small packet frozen peas

4½oz packet frozen corn

3 pickled gherkins

hard-boiled egg wedges, to
   garnish

Serve this salad for lunch or supper, or as a starter. This light and delicious salad can be prepared in advance and kept in the refrigerator. Add the dressing just before serving.

Peel the shrimp. Pick the meat from the lobster or crab, and cut it into small pieces. Cut the tomatoes into thin wedges. Mix and gently stir together the seafood, mushrooms, lettuce, and tomatoes. Blend with the asparagus and/or peas, corn, and gherkins. Chill before serving. Shake the dressing ingredients together and pour over the salad. Garnish with hard-boiled eggs, cut in wedges.

DRESSING

2 tbsp red wine vinegar

salt and white pepper

6 tbsp oil

◄ *West Coast salad*

KALE IN CREAM SAUCE
GRØNKÅL MØD FLØDE

SERVES 4–6

1lb kale

2 tsp salt

¼ cup butter

4 tbsp flour

1 cup milk

1 cup whipping or heavy cream

½ tsp freshly ground pepper

Vegetables that keep well through the winter play a large part in Danish cooking. Kale served this way makes an excellent side dish to accompany cured loin of pork, a favorite traditional dish.

Pick the tender kale leaves from their stalks, and wash thoroughly under cold running water. Shake off the water, and tear the leaves into large pieces. Cook the kale in boiling salted water for about 10–15 minutes. Drain thoroughly, then finely chop the kale.

For the sauce, melt the butter in a pan. Remove from the heat and stir in the flour. Pour in the milk and cream at the same time, whisking vigorously. Return the pan to a low heat, whisking continuously, until smooth. Season to taste. Add the finely chopped kale, and heat for a few minutes.

CARAMELIZED POTATOES

BRUNEDE KARTOFLER

SERVES 4–6

1½lb small potatoes (about 7–8)

2 tbsp sugar

2 tbsp butter

The potato came to Denmark in around 1760. These sweet-tasting potatoes were served as a treat in the olden days. Now they are part of the Danish Christmas table.

Boil the potatoes in their skins. Melt the sugar in a deep frying pan. When golden, add the butter. Peel the potatoes. Toss gently in the sugar and butter mixture until warm and well glazed.

6

DESSERTS

SOUR CREAM WAFFLES

FLOTEVAFLER

In the past, many families owned special irons made and embossed by the local blacksmiths with individual patterns. However, these waffles are just as delicious when made with a modern waffle iron.

SERVES 6

5 eggs

½ cup sugar

1 cup flour

1 tsp ground cardamom or ginger

¾ cup sour cream

¼ cup butter

Mix the eggs and sugar for about 5 minutes until fluffy. Whisk in the flour, cardamom or ginger, and sour cream. Whisk until smooth and creamy. Melt the butter, and stir it into the mixture. Set aside for 10 minutes. Cook in a waffle iron according to the manufacturer's instructions. Serve with jam, cream, or sugar.

Sour cream waffles ▶

EASTER DESSERT

PASKEDESSERT

Rich and delicious, "chocoholics" won't be able to resist this Norwegian specialty.

SERVES 4–6

½ cup butter

4oz chocolate

6 eggs, separated

½ cup sugar

1 cup ground almonds

cream, to decorate

Preheat the oven to 350°F. Melt the butter and chocolate together in a pan, stirring the mixture until it foams. Well whisk the egg yolks and sugar, then add to the chocolate mixture. Whisk the egg whites. Stir the ground almonds and finally the whisked egg whites into the mixture.

Grease a 9-inch baking pan, and sprinkle with flour. Place the mixture in the pan and stand it in a baking dish half-filled with water. Bake for about 45 minutes. Serve cold, and decorate with cream.

HONEYED PEACHES
HONUNGSPERSIKOR

Just sit back and wait for the compliments when you serve this delectable, yet simple-to-prepare, dessert.

SERVES 4–6

4 large fresh peaches, or 1 large
   can peach halves

4 tbsp honey

juice of 2 oranges

2–3 tbsp water

juice of 1 lemon, if using canned
   peaches

FILLING

4 tbsp ground almonds

4 tbsp sugar

¼ cup butter, softened

Scald, peel, halve, and remove the stone from the fresh peaches. Leave canned peaches to drain. Melt the honey in a shallow pan. Add the orange juice and water. Add the lemon juice, if necessary. Bring the syrup to the boil, and add the peach halves. Simmer until soft, turning them now and then.

Preheat the oven to 400°F. Place the peach halves, rounded side down, in an ovenproof dish, and pour the syrup over the top. Mix together the ground almonds, sugar, and softened butter. Divide the filling between the peaches. Bake the peaches until the filling is golden. Leave to cool slightly, then serve with vanilla ice cream.

BLUEBERRY PIE
MUSTIKKAPIIRAKKA

SERVES 4–6

CRUST

¾ cup butter

⅓ cup sugar (optional)

1 egg

⅓ cup whipping cream

2¼ cups flour

FILLING

2 pints blueberries

sugar to taste (optional)

1 tsp breadcrumbs or potato flour

Berries are loved by the Finns, and there are plenty for picking in the forests.

Soften the butter and add the sugar, if using. Mix in the egg thoroughly, then add the cream and flour. Mix well, but do not beat the dough. Leave the dough to stand in a cool place for 15 minutes.

Preheat the oven to 400°F. Roll out the dough into a thin sheet and transfer to a greased baking sheet, shaping a raised edge all the way around. Mix the blueberries with the sugar, if using, and the breadcrumbs or potato flour. Spread the filling on the dough. Bake until the crust is golden brown.

Blueberry pie ▶

FRUIT SALAD WITH EGG SAUCE
HIMMELSK LAPSKAUS EGGDOSIS

SERVES 4–6

2 small ripe bananas, diced or
   sliced

1½ cups seedless grapes, halved

1 large crisp apple or orange,
   diced

1½ cups hazelnuts or walnuts,
   chopped

juice of 1 lemon

EGG SAUCE

5 egg yolks

2 egg whites

5 tbsp sugar

1 tbsp cognac or rum

A refreshing fruit salad served with a creamy smooth sauce, flavored with cognac or rum.

Mix the fruit and nuts together in a bowl. Add the lemon juice to prevent the fruit from browning. Refrigerate for 20 minutes. Chill a serving dish for the sauce.

For the sauce, mix the egg yolks, egg whites, and sugar in a food processor at medium speed. When the mixture thickens, add the cognac or rum. Serve immediately in a chilled serving dish, together with the fruit.

RASPBERRY TART

BRINGEBÆR KAKE

SERVES 6

PASTRY

2 cups flour

pinch of salt

½ cup soft butter

2 tbsp sugar

1 egg yolk

LEMON CREAM

2 egg yolks

2 tbsp sugar

¾ tbsp cornstarch

generous 1 cup light cream

2 tbsp softened butter

grated rind of ¼–½ lemon

DECORATION

gelatine

1 cup water

2 tbsp sugar

juice of ½ lemon

about 2 cups fresh raspberries, or
    ½lb packet of frozen raspberries

A delicious fresh tart consisting of a thin, rich pastry shell filled with a fine lemon cream and raspberries, topped with lemon jelly. Suitable both for tea and as a dessert.

Preheat the oven to 200°F. Place the flour and salt in a bowl, then rub in the butter until the mixture resembles breadcrumbs. Stir in the sugar. Add the egg yolk, and stir until it forms a dough. Add water as necessary. Knead lightly. Use to line a shallow, straight sided flan dish, 9-inches in diameter. Bake blind for about 10 minutes, until golden. Cool slightly, then release carefully from the pan.

For the lemon cream, whisk together the egg yolks, cream, cornstarch, and sugar in a saucepan. Simmer the mixture, whisking, until the cream is thick and fluffy. Remove from the heat, add the butter, and whisk occasionally while it cools. Flavor the cold cream with the lemon rind.

Dissolve the gelatine in the water for the jelly. Add the sugar and lemon juice.

Fill the pastry shell with the lemon cream, and cover with raspberries. Pour the jelly over the top when it starts to set. Leave the tart in a cold place until serving.

Raspberry tart ▶

TROLL'S DESSERT

TROLLKREM

SERVES 4

2 egg whites

1 cup lightly sweetened apple
    sauce or ½lb (about 1½ cups)
    fresh or frozen strawberries,
    sliced

Whip up this light, creamy dessert flavored with fruit sauce or sliced strawberries and you will have a delightful end-of-meal treat in no time.

Whisk the egg whites until stiff. Add the apple sauce or strawberries. Continue whisking until the mixture is stiff and fruit and egg whites are well blended. Use an electric whisk for quick results. Serve with cream.

LEMON SOUFFLE

CITRONFROMAGE

A very light and refreshing dessert for the palate, especially after a strongly flavored main course. To serve attractively, place the soufflé in tall glasses topped with piped whipped cream and decorated with candied cherries.

SERVES 4

powdered gelatine
grated rind and juice of 1 lemon
4 eggs, separated
⅓ cup sugar
⅔ cup whipping cream

Soak the gelatine in the lemon juice. Whisk the egg whites until stiff. Dissolve the gelatine mixture in a bowl over a saucepan of hot water. Remove from the heat, and stir in the egg yolks and grated lemon rind. Fold the sugar into the egg whites, and fold gently into the lemon mixture. Pour the mixture into a glass dish, and leave to set in the refrigerator. Serve with whipped cream.

APPLES WITH MERINGUE

EPLER MED MARENGS

Set in a "sea" of custard cream, topped with meringue, this attractive dessert gives apples a new look.

SERVES 4–6

5–6 apples

½ cup sugar

¼ cup flour

1–2 eggs

1 cup cold milk

1 tsp vanilla essence

MERINGUE

4 egg whites

½ cup sugar

Preheat the oven to 350°F. Peel and core the apples. Bake for about 50 minutes, until tender. Whisk the sugar, flour, and eggs in a pan. Add the milk and vanilla essence, and cook until it thickens, stirring all the time.

Pour the custard cream into a shallow, ovenproof dish, and place the baked apples on top. For the meringue, whip the egg whites until stiff. Fold in the sugar. Cover the apples with the meringue. Sprinkle with sugar and decorate with fruit, if desired. Bake for about 30 minutes, until the meringue has set.

Apples with meringue ▶

RUM PUDDING
ROMPUDDING

Eggs given a royal treatment with a touch of rum and whipped cream. The careful preparation is well rewarded.

SERVES 4–6

1¼ cups milk

2 eggs, separated

⅓ cup sugar

gelatine

¼ cup hot water

¼ cup rum

1¼ cups whipping cream

Bring the milk to the boil. Whisk the egg yolks and sugar in a bowl for 15 minutes. Whisk in the milk, a little at a time. Return the mixture to the saucepan, and stir constantly until it thickens. Pour into a bowl for cooling.

Dissolve the gelatine in the hot water. Whisk the egg whites until stiff. Add the dissolved gelatine, rum, and whisked egg whites to the cooled mixture. Pour into a 5–cup sugared and dampened mold. Leave to set for 30 minutes in the refrigerator. Turn out, and serve decorated with whipped cream.

EASTER CHEESECAKE

PASHA

SERVES 4–6

2½lb curd cheese

1 cup butter

1 egg

3 egg yolks

⅔ cup sugar

1 cup whipping cream

1 split vanilla pod

scant ½ cup candied orange peel

scant ½ cup candied lemon peel

½ cup chopped almonds

½ cup raisins

½ tbsp ground cloves

½ tbsp ground cinnamon

2 tbsp lemon juice

20 whole ground almonds

candied cherries

Karelia is perhaps the greatest single influence on the Finnish kitchen. For centuries Karelia was the point of entry for many dishes out of the east. Some bear the unmistakable stamp of Russia. The most traditional Easter sweet is the Russian Pasha, a cheesecake.

Put the cheese into a piece of cheesecloth, and squeeze out the liquid. Melt the butter and mix with the cheese. Cream the whole egg and egg yolks with the sugar. Gradually whisk in the cream, and add the vanilla pod. Put the bowl over a pan of simmering water over a low heat. Stir the mixture until it becomes thick and creamy. Remove from the heat, and continue stirring until cooled. Remove the vanilla pod, then fold in the curd cheese. Stir in the candied peels, chopped almonds, sultanas, cloves, cinnamon, and lemon juice.

Line a 5-cup earthenware mold with a large, dampened piece of cheesecloth, and spoon in the mixture. Fold the cloth loosely over the top, and place a weight on top. Leave to stand for 1–2 days. Turn out the Pasha onto a serving dish. Decorate with almonds and candied cherries.

Easter cheesecake ▶

CRANBERRY PARFAIT

KARPALOJAADYKE

SERVES 4–6

2 egg yolks

⅔ cup sugar

⅔ cup cranberry purée

1¾ cups heavy cream

A parfait is a stylish and always successful dessert. Any berries can be used.

Whisk the egg yolks and sugar until fluffy. Stir in the cranberry purée. Whip the cream, and fold gently into the cranberry mixture. Taste to see if more sugar is needed.

Rinse a 3–5-cup mold with cold water. Pour in the mixture and freeze. To remove the parfait before serving, dip the mold into hot water for a few seconds. Serve with fresh berries and whipped cream.

PRUNE FOOL

LUUMUKIISSELI

SERVES 4–6

1lb dried prunes, pitted

6 cups water

½ cup sugar

1 stick of cinnamon

5 tbsp cornstarch

TOPPING

2 tbsp sugar

1 ¼ cups heavy or
    whipping cream

This traditional dessert is from western Finland.

Soak the prunes in cold water overnight. The next day, put the prunes and the soaking liquid in a saucepan, and add the sugar and cinnamon stick. Cook until the prunes are soft. Remove the cinnamon stick.

Thicken the prune mixture with the cornstarch mixed with a little cold water. Pour into dessert bowls, and sprinkle the 2 tbsp sugar on top. Cool to room temperature. Serve with whipped cream either on top or separately.

RHUBARB PUDDING
RABARBER COMPOTE

SERVES 4–6

2lb rhubarb

2 cups sugar

2–3 tbsp cornstarch

¼ cup water

1 tsp vanilla essence

This dessert is also called "Constitution Day Pudding," with its red and white colors representing the national flag of Denmark. On June 5, 1849, the king transferred constitutional power to the people; it is now a half-day public holiday. The rhubarb can be cooked in lemonade instead of sugar and water.

Cut the rhubarb into pieces and put into a saucepan. Spoon over most of the sugar and add enough water to cover. Cover and simmer for about 10 minutes until soft.

Mix the cornstarch with the ¼ cup water to make a smooth paste, then stir into the rhubarb. Cover and simmer until thick and clear. Stir in the vanilla essence. Pour the mixture into a serving dish, and sprinkle with the remaining sugar. Chill for 30 minutes or more. Serve with whipped cream.

Boats moored alongside the Nyhaun in Copenhagen.

RICE AND ALMOND PUDDING
RIS AL MANDE

SERVES 8–10

3¾ cups milk

¼ cup sugar

scant 1 cup long grain white rice

⅔ cup blanched almonds, halved

1 small wine glass of sherry

1–2 tsp vanilla essence

1 cup heavy cream, chilled

In the early 1800s rice was imported, so it was very expensive and reserved for special occasions only. Served hot or cold, tradition demands that a bowl is put out for Father Christmas on Christmas Eve.

Bring the milk to the boil. Add the sugar and rice, stirring occasionally. Lower the heat and simmer, uncovered, for about 25 minutes or until the rice is cooked. (To test, run a grain of rice between your thumb and forefinger; if there is no hard kernel in the center, then the rice is done.) Pour the rice immediately into a shallow bowl in order to cool it quickly.

When cool, add the almonds, sherry, and vanilla essence. Whip the cream in a chilled bowl until it thickens and holds it shape. Fold in the rice mixture. Turn the pudding into a serving dish, and chill before serving. A cold sherry or raspberry sauce is often served on top.

EGG CHEESE (BUTTERMILK CHEESE)
WNIJUUSTO

SERVES 4–6

1 gallon plus 3 cups whole milk

6½ cups buttermilk

4 eggs, separated

1 tsp salt

½ tsp sugar

Egg cheese makes a delicious dessert when served with fresh fruit or jam. It can be served hot.

Bring the milk slowly to the boil to prevent it burning. Mix the buttermilk, egg whites, salt, and sugar. Add the mixture to the hot milk, and stir well. Bring the mixture back to boil. Remove from the heat, and leave at room temperature until the mixture curdles completely.

Using a perforated spoon, transfer the cheese curd to a sieve and leave to drain for 30 minutes. Pour the curds into a bowl, add the egg yolks, and mix well.

Take a damp piece of cheesecloth and line a cheese mold. (If you do not have a cheese mold, a lined sieve can be used.) Spoon in the cheese. Fold the edges of the cloth over the top of the cheese. Leave to drain overnight. Turn out the cheese onto a serving dish. To serve hot, place in the oven at 450°F and bake for 15–20 minutes, until the top is brown.

7

CAKES, COOKIES, AND BREADS

EIVOR'S ORANGE CAKE
EIVORS APELSINKAKA

SERVES 4–6

⅔ cup butter

½ cup sugar

3 eggs

grated rind of 2 lemons

¼ cup fresh orange juice

2 cups flour, sifted with 2 tsp
baking powder

butter for greasing

breadcrumbs for coating pan

GLAZE

½ cup powdered sugar

2 tbsp fresh orange juice

a few drops of oil and yellow
food coloring

candied orange peel

◄ *Eivor's orange cake*

*This orange cake is light and airy, with a pleasant, fresh flavor.
Try it served with coffee or tea, or as a dessert accompanied
by fruit salad.*

Whisk the butter and sugar until smooth and pale. Add the eggs, one at
a time, stirring vigorously. Mix in the lemon rind and orange juice,
together with the flour. Grease a 9-inch round cake pan with the
butter, and sprinkle in the breadcrumbs. Pour the batter into the pan.
Place in a cold oven. Heat the oven to 325°–350°F and bake for 1
hour. Turn out and leave to cool under the upturned pan.

Mix the powdered sugar and orange juice to a smooth glaze. Add a
couple of drops of oil, and color the glaze light yellow with food
coloring. Spread over the cake and scatter the orange peel on top.

SPONGE CAKE WITH SOUR CREAM
KERMAKKU

SERVES 6–8

⅔ cup softened butter

1 cup sugar

3 eggs

4 cups flour

1 tsp bicarbonate of soda

1 tsp ground cinnamon

1 tsp ground cardamom or ginger

1 cup sour cream

1 tsp vanilla sugar

butter for greasing

breadcrumbs for coating pan

*Kermakku, a feather-light sponge, is made with sour cream and
delicately spiced with cinnamon, cardamom, or ginger.*

Preheat the oven to 325°F. Mix the butter and sugar until light and
creamy. Add one egg at a time, stirring constantly. Mix all the dry
ingredients together, except the vanilla sugar (sugar that has been left
with a vanilla pod to absorb the flavor) and breadcrumbs. Beat half of
the flour mixture into the creamed mixture. Whisk in the sour cream,
the rest of the flour mixture, and the vanilla sugar.

Grease a 9-inch round cake pan with the butter, and sprinkle in the
breadcrumbs. Spoon in the mixture. Bake for 50 minutes. When ready,
turn out onto a wire rack and leave to cool.

MOTHER MONSEN'S COOKIES

MOTHER MONSENS KAKE

Delicious Christmas cookies that can be prepared up to 2 weeks in advance, ready for the festive season.

MAKES 24

2 cups butter

2 cups sugar

4 eggs

2 cups flour

1 tsp vanilla essence

¼ cup chopped blanched almonds

¼ cup raisins

Preheat the oven to 350°F. Cream the butter and sugar in a bowl, or use a food processor on a low speed, until light and fluffy. Beat in one egg at a time. Add the flour and vanilla essence, then mix until smooth.

Grease a 12 x 18-inch jelly roll pan. Spread the mixture evenly in the pan, and sprinkle the surface with the almonds and raisins. Bake for 20–25 minutes, until golden brown. Leave to cool in the pan. Cut into 24 squares or triangles. To store, wrap in foil or place in an airtight container in a cool place.

Mother Monsen's cookies ▶

MAY DAY COOKIES

TIPPALEIVAT

May Day is carnival time, which starts on the eve of April 30th, called Walpurgis Night. Lots of singing and balloons are used to celebrate the arrival of spring.

MAKES 20–30

2 eggs

2 tsp sugar

1 tsp salt

1 cup milk

3½ cups flour

1–2 tsp vanilla essence

1 cup vegetable or coconut oil for frying

powdered sugar for dusting

Gently mix the eggs and sugar together. Add all the remaining ingredients, and stir until the batter is smooth. Put the batter into a piping bag fitted with a small nozzle. Heat the oil in a pan. Squeeze the batter into the pan of hot oil, making a nest-like shape. Use a metal ring in the pan, if possible, to keep the shape better during cooking. Remove the cookies when they are golden brown. Drain and cool on paper towels. When cold, dust the biscuits with powdered sugar.

CARNIVAL BUNS
FASTERLAVNSBOLLER

MAKES 8–10

DOUGH

1 tbsp dry yeast

¼ cup tepid water

2 tbsp sugar

1 egg

1 egg yolk

½ tsp salt

1 tsp ground cardamom

2 cups butter

¾ cup milk

4 cups flour, sifted

FILLING

¼lb finely chopped marzipan
  (almond paste)

2 tbsp candied mixed peel

On the Monday before Shrove Tuesday, Danish children wake up their parents early by traditionally beating them with birchwood twigs. In the afternoon they play a game called "beating a cat off the barrel," and dress up for a party afterward, when these buns are served.

Dissolve the yeast in the tepid water. Mix the sugar, egg, egg yolk, salt, cardamom, and ⅓ cup of the butter. Add to the dissolved yeast. Warm the milk. Add the lukewarm milk to the mixture. Mix in the flour and the rest of the butter. Knead the dough until smooth and pliable. Add the marzipan and mixed peel. Chill for 10 minutes.

Roll out the chilled dough to ¼-inch thickness. Cut into 2–3-inch squares, and put onto a greased baking tray.

Leave to rise until doubled in size. Preheat the oven to 425°F. Bake for 12 minutes, until golden brown. Sprinkle with sifted powdered sugar.

Carnival buns ▶

NORWEGIAN WHOLEWHEAT BREAD
NORSK HELKORNSBRØD

MAKES 1 LOAF AND 10 ROLLS OR 2 LOAVES

1¼ lb wholewheat kernels

2¼ cups skimmed milk

4 tbsp fresh yeast

2 tbsp salt

1 tbsp oil

½ cup cottage cheese

8½ cups wholewheat flour

1½ cups white flour

crushed wheat for coating

Anybody who has traveled in Norway must have envied the Norwegians their fine bread. Here is one example.

Soak the wholewheat kernels for about 1 hour in lukewarm water. Heat the milk to body temperature, and stir the yeast into the liquid.

Add the salt, oil, cottage cheese, wholemeal flour, well-drained wheat kernels and, finally, the white flour. Knead the dough until smooth. Leave to rise for 30 minutes.

Shape into one loaf and 10 rolls, or 2 loaves. Roll everything in crushed wheat. Place the loaf in a greased 2lb loaf tin and the rolls on a greased baking sheet, and leave to rise until doubled in size. Preheat the oven to 400°F. Bake the loaf for about 40–45 minutes. Bake the rolls at 425°F for about 20 minutes.

CAKE FROM JÄMTLAND
SÖNDAGSKAKA FRÅN JÄMTLAND

SERVES 4

4 eggs, separated

3 tbsp sugar

5 tbsp flour

grated rind of 1 lemon

1¼ cups heavy cream or sour
   cream, or 1 cup plain yogurt

butter for greasing

breadcrumbs for coating pan

*The sharp lemon flavor and smooth, creamy texture of this
cake makes a perfect contrast to the accompanying
jam or fruit.*

Preheat the oven to 350°F. Whisk the egg yolks with the sugar and
flour. Add the lemon rind. Whip the cream, and stir it into the egg
mixture. If using yogurt, just mix it in. Whisk the egg whites into peaks,
and fold into the mixture. Mix well, but do not stir or the batter might
sink. Pour the mixture into a greased and breadcrumbed 9-inch cake
pan. Bake for 35–40 minutes. Do not open oven door during the first
25 minutes. Serve the cake freshly baked as dessert with any kind of
jam, or berries and soft fruit.

ALMOND CONE CAKE

K R A N S E K A K E

SERVES 6–8

4½ cups almonds

2¼ cups powdered sugar

3 egg whites

ICING

scant 1 cup powdered sugar

½ egg white

1 tsp white wine vinegar

A traditional delicacy for Norwegian National Day, May 17th. Almond cone cake is based on just 3 ingredients: almonds, powdered sugar, and egg whites. Decorate the finished cone with marzipan fruits for a special treat.

Blanch and skin the almonds, then leave to dry thoroughly. Grind to a paste. Place in a bowl, and mix with the powdered sugar. Add half of the egg whites (unwhipped), and work the dough well. Place the bowl over a pan of gently simmering water, and stir in the remaining egg white. Stir continuously until the dough is lukewarm.

Preheat the oven to 325°F. Grease and flour various sized ring molds. These should graduate regularly in size. Ideal sizes are 3-inches, 5-inches, 7-inches, and 9-inches.

While the dough is still warm, spoon into a piping bag with a large nozzle, and pipe into the ring molds. Place the rings on trays with the various sizes within each other. Bake until light brown.

For the icing, sift the powdered sugar and stir sufficient into the egg white with the vinegar until it forms firm peaks. Spoon into a piping bag fitted with a small piping nozzle. To assemble the cake, place the largest ring on a serving plate and decorate with a zigzag pattern of icing. Place the next size ring on top, and repeat the process until all of the rings are in position. The height of the cake will depend on the number of rings made.

A stunning midsummer pole on the Aland Islands of Finland.

LEMON CAKE

CITRONKAK

SERVES 6–8

scant 2 cups flour

scant ½ cup butter

2 tbsp sugar

CREAM

2 eggs

2 tbsp flour

½ tsp baking powder

grated rind of ½ lemon

sugar for sifting

The lemon flavor of the cream topping gives just the right balance to the plain but very light, delicate texture of the cake.

Preheat the oven to 325°F. Mix the flour, butter, and sugar to a dough. Press out the dough into a greased 9-inch cake pan. Let the dough settle. Bake for about 20 minutes. Meanwhile, mix together the ingredients for the cream, except the sugar. Pour the mixture over the cake base in the tin. Bake for a further 25 minutes. Turn out, and let the cake cool. Sift the sugar on top and serve.

Lemon cake ▶

ALMOND CAKES

MANDELBAKKELS

MAKES 16–20

1 cup flaked almonds

butter for greasing

2 eggs

¾ cup sugar

2–3 bitter almonds, grated

1¼ cups plain flour

⅓ cup butter, melted

Easy to make, these little cakes, with their delicate almond flavor, are a mouthwatering treat. For a special occasion, soak the cakes in sherry or freshly squeezed orange juice with a little rum added, then top with whipped cream.

Preheat the oven to 400°F. Toast the flaked almonds lightly, then crumble or chop finely. Leave to cool. Carefully grease 16–20 small cake molds or patty pan with soft butter, and scatter them with the chopped almonds.

Whisk the eggs until frothy, add the sugar, and whisk to a fluffy mixture. Mix in the grated almonds, flour, and the cooled butter. Stir gently to prevent the mixture collapsing. Divide the mixture between the molds, and place on a baking sheet. Bake for 15 minutes. Turn out and leave to cool under the upturned molds.

BROWN MUFFINS

BRUNA MUFFINS

There is nothing more tempting than freshly baked muffins with your coffee. These muffins have a character of their own, and are good for freezing, too.

MAKES 15–20

½ cup butter

scant 1 cup corn syrup

2 eggs

3 tbsp orange marmalade

3 tbsp cold, strong coffee

3 tbsp almonds or hazelnuts, chopped

scant 2 cups flour

2 tsp baking powder

1 tsp ground cinnamon

½ cup light cream

Preheat the oven to 425°F. Grease 12 muffin or deep patty pans. Work the butter until soft and creamy. Mix in the syrup. Stir in one egg at a time. Add the marmalade and coffee. Mix the almonds or hazelnuts with the flour, baking powder, and cinnamon. Stir the flour mixture into the batter, alternating with the cream. Divide the mixture between the pans. Bake for about 10 minutes. Leave to cool under a cloth.

Brown muffins ▶

BISCUIT CAKE

ISCHOKLADKAKA

Biscuit cake, also called ice chocolate cake, is delicious and no cooking is needed.

SERVES 4–6

1 cup plus 2 tbsp coconut butter

2 eggs

¾ cup powdered sugar, sifted

¾ cup cocoa powder, sifted

½ cup semisweet biscuits, crushed

15–20 chocolate pieces (optional)

Melt the coconut butter in a saucepan and leave to cool. Line an oblong cake pan with waxed paper. Whisk the eggs and powdered sugar until creamy. Stir the cocoa powder into the egg mixture. Add the fat and stir vigorously. Pour a thin layer of the mixture into the cake pan and place a layer of biscuits over the top. Keep repeating the layering, finishing with cocoa mixture. Leave to cool overnight (not in the freezer).

Remove the cake, and place it on a serving dish. Decorate with chocolate pieces, and serve by cutting thin slices.

VANILLA RINGS

VANILLE KRANSE

MAKES 20 RINGS

1 cup butter

1 cup sugar

1 egg

2 tsp vanilla essence

¾ cup ground almonds

3 cups flour

◄ *Vanilla rings*

Danish cookies and cakes are both rich and artistic. They deserve the place of honor on the coffee table.

Preheat the oven to 350°F. Cream the butter and sugar in a bowl, or use a food processor on a low speed, until light and fluffy. Beat in the egg, then the vanilla essence, almonds, and flour. Put the paste into a piping bag fitted with a star-shaped nozzle. Pipe 2-inch rings onto a greased baking tray. Bake for about 8–9 minutes.

LENT BUNS

LASKIAISPULLA

MAKES 20

2¼ cups milk

2 eggs

scant 1 cup sugar

2 scant tbsp fresh yeast

3 tsp salt

1 tbsp ground cardamom

1 cup butter or
   scant 1 cup vegetable oil

9 cups flour

egg yolk for glazing

FILLING

1¼ cups cream

1 tbsp sugar

HOT CHOCOLATE

7½ cups milk

4 tbsp cocoa powder, sifted

2 tbsp sugar

A traditional Finnish Lenten meal would be green pea soup, pig's feet, and these Lent Buns. All the bun ingredients should be at room temperature to shorten the rising time of the dough.

Warm the milk until it is lukewarm. Beat the eggs and sugar until creamy. Add the milk, yeast, salt, and cardamom. (If oil is used instead of butter, add it now.) Beat in the flour and butter vigorously; lots of air will help the dough to rise well. Knead the dough on a well-floured board. Knead until it separates easily from your hands. Cover the dough with a cloth, and leave to rise until doubled in size. Make 20 balls, and place on a greased baking tray. Cover with a cloth, and leave to rise in a warm place for 30 minutes. Preheat the oven to 375°F.

Brush the balls with beaten egg yolk. Bake for about 30 minutes, until golden brown. Remove and leave to cool on a wire rack.

For the filling, whip the cream and sugar. Cut the buns in half, and fill them with the whipped cream.

For the hot chocolate, boil the milk and add the cocoa powder and sugar, whisking vigorously. Place the buns in individual bowls, and pour the hot chocolate over them just before serving.

INDEX